I CANNOT
GO BACK

I CANNOT GO BACK

JIMMY SNOW

with Jim and Marti Hefley

LOGOS INTERNATIONAL
Plainfield, New Jersey

CONTENTS

JOHNNY CASH

MY FRIEND, JIMMY SNOW

In many ways Jimmy Snow's spiritual life parallels that of the Apostle Paul. He rejected God's true way, ridiculed and laughed at the ones who tried to point him to Christ and almost destroyed himself in feasting on every evil thing the world had to offer.

Jimmy's conversion eighteen years ago was a road-to-Damascus kind of conversion. In this book he tells how the scales of spiritual blindness fell from his eyes one night and how his life was turned completely around and given to God's service. His life is a textbook case on the power of the saving love of Christ over the destructive influence of Satan.

His work, his dedication and the bountiful harvest of souls delivered over to God's side through his divinely a-nointed ministry is a beacon of proof to a lost world that God will touch you and save you no matter who or no matter what you are.

A lot of questions are answered here in his own words, a lot of misconceptions about himself are clarified. Light is shed on his character and on his mind. Some of his revelations may surprise you, some of it sounds like a public confession, but the humbled-at-the-feet-of-Jesus attitude of my friend and brother, Jimmy Snow, will inspire you.

Johnny Cash

Preface

John Pugh put it this way in *Nashville!* magazine. "He has been praised and damned, cussed and discussed, sworn by and sworn at by practically everyone who has had any experience with him." And Pugh quoted someone in the country music community as saying, "Snow stories are almost as common as Polish jokes" in Nashville.

People have a right to their opinions. And I have a right to mine.

This is my story—the story critics and friends say they are waiting to read.

Some will like it. Some won't. Some will praise God. Some may wring their hands in despair.

I have tried to tell it honestly and candidly, warts and all. How else could I show the mercy and the miracle-working power of God?

The following names are fictitious and used for the protection of the privacy of certain non-public individuals: Joyce Harrod, a girlfriend. Suzy and Harry Caldwell, operators of Caldwell's Beer Tavern. Jerry and Burl, two boyhood friends. Brother Sharp, the preacher who failed me. The Greenbriar Night Club and its former manager, Billy Wetzel. The Arab guide, Assad.

But the facts and events are as I have lived and understood them.

I have tried to be fair and accurate. I believe I have been harder on myself than anyone else. Above all, I have tried to magnify the grace of God.

All praise to Him for saving a sinner like me.

I CANNOT GO BACK

1
Encounter!

It was near one o'clock that cold November night back in 1957 when I staggered through the chain-link gate that opens ·to the driveway of my parents' modest red brick house. I was so drunk I couldn't have read the letters in the metal arch spelling out RAINBOW RANCH even if I had wanted to. The country music fans in the never ending stream of tour buses might get a thrill out of seeing the home of Hank Snow, but it sure didn't impress me.

So what if he was Number One in the current Country Music Popularity Pool, outranking Webb Pierce, Johnny Cash and Hank Williams. I was sick of being "the son of" Hank Snow. I wanted to be me, not just walk in my father's shadow. I had made some progress in that direction, appearing with Lawrence Welk on national television a few weeks previously. But that trip to Hollywood hadn't brought the satisfaction I had expected any more than the governor of Tennessee's personal recommendation to Elia Kazan's famous Actor's Studio.

As I lurched toward the side door of the house it mattered little to my fuzzy brain that my show dates were increasing and that my record sales were picking up. I might have fooled some people into thinking there was hope for me after all, but I couldn't kid myself. I knew I was a loser. A pillhead and a drunk, I couldn't stay sober twenty-four hours.

I climbed the concrete stairs hoping I wouldn't wake my mother. Dad was out of the city on a show so I didn't have to worry about him hearing me, but I didn't want to face mother. So far I had been able to keep from my sweet, naive mother the fact that her precious only child was a boozehound.

Opening the door, I saw a dim light shining from beneath her door. She must have been reading or watching television. I staggered toward my room as stealthily as possible, groggily reminding myself, "Mushn't wake mama. Mushn't wake mama."

I entered my room and fell across the bed relieved that my secret was still safe, and yet hating myself for deceiving my loving, trusting parent. I was so totally disgusted with myself that I didn't care if I lived or died.

Fans would have found that hard to believe. At twenty-one I had everything the world says should make you happy. Youth, money, a famous name. Friends like Elvis Presley, Tommy Sands, Bill Haley, and other big names in the new rock-and-roll craze. A beautiful girl who had said she would marry me. Opportunities opening to make it big on my own.

And nothing.

I moaned aloud as I rolled over, hating myself. My wretched, miserable, empty self. I seemed to have a gift for ruining everything I touched. Booze and pills had me totally enslaved. I was so hopelessly bound that even dad had given up on me.

That still hurt. It had been a year since he had called me into his office to show me his insurance policies and his will that he had spread out across his desk. Stone-faced, he had indicated the lines marked "beneficiaries" and told me my name had been removed.

It wasn't being cut off from his money that hurt, but the realization that I had shattered all his dreams for me. Ever since I made my first stage appearance at two-and-a-half he had been teaching, molding, grooming me, his only child, for the big moment when he could present me as the newest member of the Grand Ole Opry. Instead I was "Jimmie Rodgers Snow—The Bum."

I couldn't blame him for disinheriting me. He and mother felt that if I was determined to ruin my life at least I wasn't going to do it with their money. I'd always have room and board, dad promised, but no money to waste.

I glanced up at the wagon-wheel headboard that gleamed at me accusingly. The bed and the rest of the furniture in my room had been custom-made of varnished pine in Texas. Handcrafted with wooden pegs, there wasn't a nail anywhere in it. Nothing too good for the son of Hank Snow. I snorted at the irony of the thought.

"Nothing too good . . . " and yet I spent my nights boozing myself senseless. Seducing women and then robbing them while they were drunk. Popping pills to break the tension. I was sick of my life, but I couldn't turn it around.

I wanted desperately to change. Deep inside I felt a crushing guilt and a desperate yearning to really know God. I had seen the movie, *The Ten Commandments*, seven times and had been both frightened and challenged. Frightened by God's judgment on sin, for I had broken every commandment except the sixth. But challenged by God's leader, Moses. For buried deep in the befuddled recesses of my brain was a gnawing intuition that God wanted me to be a preacher like Moses.

A painful, ironic laugh escaped at the thought of that impossible dream. Me, a preacher giving forth God's message. Telling other people how to live. I wasn't worthy to kiss the knob on a church door.

*In my early years it was Jimmie, but more recently it's become Jimmy.

I swung my feet over the side of the bed and sat there staring blankly into the future. Slowly I pulled off my shirt and shoes and socks. Then I reached into my pants pocket and pulled out the snub-nosed Smith and Wesson revolver I always carried.

The light flashed tauntingly off the cold steel of the deadly weapon. This wasn't the first time I had contemplated suicide. A few weeks before I had swallowed a handful of barbiturates, only to awaken to the realization that I had failed in yet another endeavor. Then I tried driving my car 80-90-100-105 miles an hour, intending to crash into a telephone pole. Each time I swerved back onto the road. I just didn't have the guts.

The gun seemed to make my fingers itch. As if it were daring me to use it. I stuck the barrel in my mouth, detemined to show myself that I could pull the trigger. I still couldn't do it. I didn't have the nerve.

I threw the gun on the bed and wobbled toward the door. I had to get away. Away from myself. Away from my sin.

I stepped into the bitter cold night barefoot and shirtless. The frigid air came as a shock to my lungs, but did little to clear my foggy brain. I started running. Running blindly into the darkness. Somehow I got to the mail box and there I fell on my face on the cold ground and began crying out to God.

"God, I'm miserable. God, I'm hopeless. God, I'm no good. God, nobody can help me. You've got to help me. God, if you're really there, help me. Please, God. Please. I'm sorry. Oh, God, forgive me. Tell me that you love me. Please, God. Oh, God. Please, God."

The words came rushing out in a torrent. Louder and louder. Porch lights came on across the street. The neighbors must have figured I was coming home from another drunk.

"Please, God, hear me. Forgive me. Jesus, help me. Save me. Oh, please. Please."

I must have prayed an hour in the freezing cold. I would have stayed there all night, I was so desperate. But sometime, somehow, I reached out in faith and complete dependence on

God. All I know is that my mind cleared and I was filled with an overflowing peace. I knew my past had been forgiven. That my future belonged to Him. God had not only accepted me; He was going to use me in His service. Like Moses, I was going to be His spokesman.

Totally unaware of the numbness of my feet, I dashed back into the house, shouting, "Mother, I'm changed, I've met God. I'm different. I'm forgiven. And I'm going to be a preacher."

My poor mother stared at me as if I were a ghost. She didn't know what to think of me. The novel she had been reading slipped to her lap and she sighed, "Son, you're going to have a nervous breakdown yet."

I returned to my room too excited to sleep. I had to share this experience with someone who would understand. I immediately thought of Brother Alford, the pastor of the Assembly of God church I had attended with an old girlfriend.

I slipped on my shirt and shoes and, leaving my gun forgotten on my bed, hurried outside. I jumped into the pickup and backed up straight as an arrow out of the driveway. In a couple of minutes I was pounding on his door.

The tousle headed preacher greeted me in his nightclothes. "God has saved me!" I announced like a wild man. "And He's called me to be a preacher!"

"Well, praise the Lord, Jimmie," Brother Alford exclaimed, coming instantly awake. "Praise the Lord! Come on in. Tell me how it happened."

We talked for a long time. Sometime before daylight I got back in the truck and drove home. As I pulled into the driveway I glanced over at the mailbox. Tears filled my eyes as I looked at what had become for me a hallowed spot. My mind was still whirling, but I was positive of two things: God had given me a new life and He had called me to preach. There could be no denying what had happened. I'd never be the same. I could not go back.

2
A Boy in Nova Scotia

Maybe I ought to start at the beginning and explain that my growing up was different from most country music and rock-and-roll entertainers. I didn't come from a preacher's family, as Roy Acuff did; do a stint as a teen-age preacher, as Conway Twitty did; or get started singing in a church, as Elvis Presley, Hank Williams, and many others did.

Nor did I grow up in a "y-all" and "shore nuff" southern town of grits and gravy.

Not by a long shot. I came from Halifax, Nova Scotia, the poetic home of the French Canadians whom Longfellow immortalized in his poem *Evangeline*. My only religious connection was with the Anglican Church.

My dad, Clarence E. "Hank" Snow, like many others on the Grand Ole Opry, is Scotch-Irish. We believe, but can't prove, that he's a direct descendant from a Snow who came over on the Mayflower, and whose family later migrated north to the island peninsula that hangs in the Atlantic about halfway between Cape Cod and Newfoundland.

Dad's people were hard-working farmers, lumbermen and

fishermen who brightened their lives by singing story-telling ballads to the accompaniment of native instruments. Their distant Scotch-Irish relatives to the south carried the same music with them as they migrated west into the Appalachian and Cumberland mountains. The lyrics and melodies were born of loneliness, romance, family bonds, heartbreak, and hope of heaven—the stuff from which pioneer life was made. From this legacy of folk ballads came the country music of today.

Dad's immediate family might have been professionals had they lived thirty years later. His father and one of his sisters were good singers and his mother could memorize music as she played along. His mother did play the piano accompaniment for silent films in theaters.

Dad really lived many of the hard-time songs he would become famous for in the fifties. He was sort of a "Nobody's Child" after his parents broke up and his mother remarried. When he was only twelve, two of his sisters were taken to live in foster homes and a third went to work in a factory. He helped support the two younger sisters by working as a cabin boy on a schooner.

Dad met mother in Halifax, the provincial capital and big seaport that serves the North Atlantic. Mother's lineage is Dutch-English-Irish. Her maiden name was "Aalders," always spelled with two Dutch "a's." That makes me Dutch-English-Scotch-Irish.

They were married during the depth of the Great Depression. When mother became pregnant with me, dad was tramping the streets looking for work. They seldom knew where the next meal was coming from.

Unable to afford hospital care, they intended for me to be born at home. But when labor started that frigid February morning, complications developed and dad had to call the Salvation Army Hospital. The ambulance attendants carried mother down from the two-room walkup apartment in a blanket. The stairs were too narrow for a stretcher.

Because the twenty-six-dollar charge for the difficult breech birth was written off, dad has always had a warm heart for the Salvation Army. In the years since he's paid the bill and much more.

They were living then on Artz Street about a block from the waterfront. The weather was usually cloudy and damp with chilling fog. I cried a lot in the bureau drawer that served for my bed, and mother worried I'd catch pneumonia and die. Instead I broke out with red blotches and a high fever.

The doctor pronounced it a streptococcus infection called erysipelas, and said only a new wonder drug called penicillin might save me. "I don't know whether we can get it in Halifax or not," he said. "We'll try."

His nurse began calling a list of pharmacies while my parents waited anxiously. "There's one more possibility," she said. "Keep your fingers crossed."

They had it. My life was saved.

After making a quick recovery, I showed my first indication of non-conformity. I learned to crawl backwards. This was too slow, so I tried rolling across the room. When I learned to talk, I called mother "Min" (for Minnie) and her mother "mom." Probably because I heard mother's brothers calling them by these names.

Dad lived and breathed country music. The year I was born he was singing on a local radio station, and for any group that wanted entertainment. A few months later he cut his first record for RCA Victor.

The pay was hardly enough to keep me in baby shoes. To feed his family, he taught himself to give guitar lessons, staying a lesson ahead of his students.

He had to go out and look for prospects. When he brought one home, mother shooed me in the kitchen and kept me quiet while dad taught the lesson. Then when he finished, she'd grab the fifty cents and run out and buy food.

Our one luxury was a small electric radio—"a dollar down and a dollar when you catch me," dad remembers. My earliest memories are of dad twirling its dial for country music.

Dad's idol was the late Jimmie Rodgers, now honored as the "father" of country music. Dad liked his mellow resonant voice and "blue yodel" and was also inspired by his hard road to success.

Rodgers was a skinny railroad brakeman who entertained his fellow workers during lunch breaks. When tuberculosis forced him to quit the railroad at twenty-eight, he struck out for the North Carolina mountains and got a job singing on a radio station in Asheville. This job didn't last long and he worked as a city detective until record promoter Ralph Peer came along. Peer recorded Rodgers and the Carter Family of Maces Spring, Virginia, the same week, marking two milestones in country music.

Jimmie Rodgers' first record royalty was $27.43. Half a year later he was making $2,000 a month and when he died in 1933, three years before I was born, his annual income was over $100,000.

Dad and a host of other stars to come—Gene Autry, Bob Wills, Eddy Arnold, Red Foley, Hank Williams, and T. Texas Tyler, to name a few—built their style around the lonesome railroad songs of the tubercular brakeman.

But dad did more than adopt Jimmie Rodgers' style. He named me, his first-born, for his hero. And he took his first stage title, "The Yodeling Ranger," from a song which Jimmie Rodgers composed in appreciation for being named an honorary Texas Ranger. Later, when dad's voice deepened, he called himself "The Singing Ranger."

It was a foregone conclusion that dad and I would be a father-son team. At the tender age of two, as soon as I could carry a tune, he stood me atop two Coca-Cola cases and announced, "Ladies and gentlemen, may I present my son, Jimmie Rodgers Snow, named after my idol in country music." With dad accompanying on the guitar, I belted out, "Jesus Loves Me." I must have learned it in the Anglican Sunday school, although I don't remember going. Dad was so proud of me he recorded my performance for posterity.

Assured I would be a stage success, he dressed me in a little cowboy suit and added "Playmate, Come Out and Play With Me" to my repertoire. The charity hall crowd cheered when I sang and oohed, "He's soooooo cute." My "act" became a regular part of dad's show. At six dad took me with him to Montreal for a recording session with RCA. I wasn't impressed at all by the ponderous machines. I got rather tired of hearing dad sing the same song over and over. Finally the producer scrounged some toys and told me to go play in the corner.

By this time dad was making tours all through eastern Canada, using the home of mother's parents in the Halifax suburb of Fairview as a base. I liked living with grampa and "mom" and my six uncles who weren't much older than I.

The two-story frame house was on a hill and overlooked the harbor where the big munition ships were anchored. During those early years in grade school I missed many days of school because of appearing on shows that dad had nearby. I couldn't have cared less.

What I really enjoyed most was wintertime sports. Tobogganing down hills at breakneck speed, playing hockey on frozen ponds, and ice skating on Chocolate Lake. Those childhood evenings on the lake still light up in my memory. Hundreds of skaters whipping around the ice, waving long slender oil-dipped cat-o'-nine-tails for torches. The streams of fire ribboning the darkness turned the lake into a glittering fairyland.

My uncles were like big brothers. I thought the oldest were the strongest and bravest boys in the world. Especially Uncle

John who resembled Errol Flynn. I watched him stand in a corner and whip six men his size. I saw him knock a guy across the room with such force that he carried the door out with him. I watched goggle-eyed when he held up the front end of a Buick while another of my uncles changed the tire.

Fairview wasn't very large, maybe five thousand. Most kids had the run of the town. When I wasn't with my uncles, I was chasing around to find some action. Marbles. Fights. Poker and craps, two games I learned before I was six. Always trying to learn from older kids.

One night, I noticed teenagers going into the woods and followed them to an old clubhouse they had built from lumber scraps. Slipping up to the wall, I peeked through a crack. It looked like some kind of a wrestling match between boys and girls on mattresses scattered across the dirt floor.

I got bored and left. Two or three nights later I sneaked back. Someone spotted me this time and invited me inside. I was just a little kid, too young to feel any sexual desire, but I watched out of curiosity. And I never told any of the adults that their kids were having sex orgies in the old shack back in the woods.

Not all of my time was spent observing the practices of older teens. My pal was Uncle Vic who was just two years older than I. After my four oldest uncles went off to war, Vic developed St. Vitus dance, a nerve disease. The doctor who treated him prescribed the wrong medicine. Vic's body was so affected that he had to avoid sunlight for a year.

He got in the habit of sleeping in the daytime and staying awake at night. With my four oldest uncles gone to war, I spent most of my time with Vic.

We heard a radio warning that a German submarine had slipped into the harbor. The authorities thought enemy soldiers might try to come ashore and spy out the area for possible sabotage. If a citizen saw strangers, he shouldn't be alarmed. Friendly forces would be close by.

Naturally Vic and I hung out the windows that night looking. About 2 A.M., I whispered, "Psst. Four guys in uniforms are coming up the street." When they got closer we saw the German markings and held our breath until they passed. We never heard if they were captured.

Understandably, Vic and I developed vivid imaginations. His two brothers knew this and convinced us a headless man was hiding out in the back yard privy. We became too frightened to use it at night. Instead we resorted to the bedroom window.

One evening the adults were sitting at the kitchen table drinking coffee when "mom" noticed water trickling down the side of the house. They knew it wasn't raining and came up and thrashed us. But we still wouldn't go to the outhouse after dark.

Sunday was just another day. There were only a couple of churches in Fairview and families were either Anglican or Catholic. If the Anglicans were having a party, Vic and I might go. This was after his health improved.

There was one party when I was nine that I'll never forget. It was on Wednesday evening, July 18, 1945. Germany and Italy had surrendered in May and victory over Japan was imminent. The service boys were coming home and everybody was in a festive mood.

Tables were decorated and set up on the church lawn that adjoined the cemetery, a historical landmark in Canada. In 1917 a French ammo ship had blown up in the harbor, touching off explosions that killed almost two thousand people. The ship's anchor had been blown five miles, landing in the Anglican cemetery. The anchor was still sticking up among tombstones.

With the harbor serving once more as the Allied ammunition depot for the North Atlantic region, people had feared it might blow up again. But now that the war was so close to being over nobody thought much about the reminder that lay half buried in the cemetery and the possibility of a repeat performance.

Vic and I were standing around waiting for the supper to start. My mother and an aunt had gone to the post office to mail letters and would be returning shortly. Dad was keeping a show date in New Brunswick.

The time was about five-thirty. In back of us, the sun was still high above the "murmuring pines and hemlock" which Longfellow wrote about in *Evangeline*. The ammunition ships rode gently on the blue waters below us.

Suddenly Vic nudged me on the shoulder and pointed. "Hey, that ship is on fire!"

I was swinging my head to look when the sky turned red and a force lifted me into the branches of a tree. Cakes and pies and pieces of chicken were flying and people were screaming and running away from the direction of the explosion. They were surging across a field in blind, frantic panic, desperately looking for a place of safety.

My grandfather helped me down from the tree and I joined the others trying to escape the living nightmare. As I ran I could feel the heat from behind and see the red sky in front. Boom! Another explosion knocked me to the ground. I jumped up and started running again only to be thrown down by yet a third explosion.

Pillars of fire were shooting 150 feet into the air. Rockets were exploding and showers of shrapnel were raining from the sky. Terrified, Vic and I dove into an old storm cellar near an abandoned house. We could hear people crying, praying, calling for loved ones. It was like the apocalypse.

We huddled together in our dank sanctuary, fear erasing all sense of time. Finally an uneasy calm settled over the scene despite the continuing explosions in the harbor. At last my mother found us and we made our way home. The civil defense authorities gave permission to return long enough to get some supplies, then we were to seek shelter in the more secure bomb shelters that had been built in the woods on the other side of town.

The windows and front door panel had been blown out of my grandparents' home, grim reminders of the need to hurry to the underground shelters that had been built because the Allied shipping and ammunition depot had made Halifax a vulnerable location.

With thousands of others we squeezed into the gloomy shelter. Children were crying. Everyone was frightened. And throughout the long night the explosions continued. The most terrifying thought was that the main magazine might be next. Everyone knew that if it blew, Halifax would be blown from the map.

But that dreaded blast never came and after three days we were allowed to go home. A radio report told us what saved the town.

A brave fireman had gone down into the hull and turned valves to flood the magazine. He had done that knowing that he would certainly be drowned. Had the magazine holding fifty thousand tons of T.N.T. exploded there would probably have been hundreds of deaths and major property damage. But only the stoker and a sentry had died and about 100 were injured.

Dad had heard about the explosions over the radio. He couldn't call because the telephone lines were down. Not until he got home did he know that we had escaped unharmed.

"Boy, were we lucky," I told Vic.

"Yeah," he agreed, "real lucky."

I didn't consider that God had spared my life a second time, or for what purpose.

3
Nashville Bound

Show business had become a way of life for our family. Performing and being the center of attention was regular stuff for me. I was the icing on dad's cake, the little kid in the cute cowboy suit who stole the show and I could tell by the proud look on dad's face that he was pleased.

Mother had charge of the bookings and box office. Sometimes she'd go ahead while we were finishing an engagement to arrange shows in the next town. But she was always there when we opened, selling tickets and programs, keeping the popcorn girl in line, and checking to see that my outfit was clean just before time to go on.

Dad handled the talent. He set the perfect example. I never saw a smudge on his white cowboy hat, yellow kerchief, and tailored white suit. Nor did his boots ever reflect less than a mirror finish.

He expected me to look the same. There was no excuse for coming on stage in a soiled outfit. None. The one time it happened, he taught me a lesson I never forgot.

We were in a small town in New Brunswick. I was dressed like a dandy and waiting for the show to start when two boys lured me away from the tent to the bank of a little creek. When I got near the water, one shoved me in.

When dad saw me muddy and dripping wet, he jerked a dress from a drawer and ordered me to change. Then he took me to the track that ran before the grandstand and made me parade in front of the crowd.

The audience roared with laughter as I trudged across the track, my face beet red. Back inside I got a whipping and changed for the regular performance. Never again did I get my outfit dirty.

For dad the show always had to go on. Moods and minor illnesses didn't count. And the show had to begin on time. Not a minute late.

He didn't have to tell me twice to memorize my songs and enunciate each syllable letter perfect. That was the way he did it. I never heard him mush a word or miss a strum on the guitar. He told me what to sing and when. But he could never make me comfortable on stage.

When he'd tell me to "say hello to the audience," all I could manage was, "Good evening, ladies and gentlemen." Then I'd sing what he wanted me to.

I can understand dad's toughness. Show business was not only his first love, but his only way of climbing out of the pit of poverty. And he wanted me to succeed as well. Like other fathers of the Depression era, he didn't want his child to pass through the same tribulation.

Dad realized he couldn't stay in Canada and make it to the big time. The stations were not powerful enough and record sales were inadequate.

He could only make it in the United States. It was not a matter of patriotism, but economic survival and success. And dad was determined to make it to the top.

The country music shows on big stations beckoned. The "National Barn Dance" on WLS-WGN (Chicago). The "Midwestern Hayride" on WLW (Cincinnati). The "Big D Jamboree" on KRLD (Dallas). The WWVA "Jamboree" (Wheeling, West Virginia). The super-powerful outlets across the Mexican border where the Carter Family was winning a name. And the "Grand Ole Opry" on WSM (Nashville) which was sounding better every Saturday night. Already performers were using other stations as stepping stones to the Opry.

WWVA (Wheeling) was closest. Dad had friends there. Just before Christmas '46 we loaded up our old Buick and headed south toward coal-mining country.

While dad was getting started we lived with a couple named Big Slim and Ruby who had a little ranch house just outside of Wheeling. We did a few shows with them.

Big Slim was full Indian, tall, dark, and ruddy-skinned. He was fantastic on his black-and-white trick stallion, Flash. He could bring the house down with his rendition of "Don't Fence Me In" and other western songs. But what grabbed me the most was his whip act with his beautiful blonde wife.

Ruby stood a full twenty feet away with a cigarette extending from her red lips. Big Slim cracked his whip a couple of times, then zipped it across the stage and cut the cigarette in two.

The audience always gasped and, the first time I saw it, I almost fell over. But that wasn't all. For the finale he wrapped the whip around her neck and popped the rest of the cigarette from her mouth.

Slim could be mean when he was drinking. We could always tell when he was mad at Ruby because, when he did the neck trick, he would flip a little gash along her temple. She never whimpered or let on; just stood there and smiled while the blood trickled down her neck. But she'd let him have it when they got off stage.

From Slim and Ruby's we moved to a trailer park across the

state line in Pennsylvania, where several other country-music families lived.

Our next abode was the Wheeling Hotel. While there I developed a mad crush on the Davis Sisters, blind twin singers who lived downstairs. When they'd come home from the radio station, I'd run down and butter them up. I never could decide which I liked better.

Then we moved to a third floor apartment of a house on Wheeling Island on the Ohio River. It seemed like a nice place until spring when the floodwaters began rising. About the time the water was reaching alarming heights, I came down with the measles. As the water level climbed, the people on the first floor were evacuated, then those on the second floor were taken out in boats. Mother wouldn't leave for fear I'd catch pneumonia.

Dad was at WWVA and couldn't come. We'd hear him sing on the radio, then he'd call and ask mother, "How much higher?" She'd run and look out the back door to see how many steps the water was from our door.

I'd jump out of bed and run to a window to watch the trees and lumber floating by. "Jimmie, you get back into bed," she'd shout and I'd dive back under the covers. Then she'd pick up the phone and report to dad. We never did have to move out.

After I recovered, I sang on dad's program. I got stacks of fan letters, mostly from adults predicting that if I kept on, someday I'd be a big star. I wasn't thrilled. Show business to me was just a part of life.

That summer dad went on tour. He took mother and me back to Halifax, which I didn't mind at all, and went back to Pennsylvania and bought a black-and-white trick pinto named Shawnee. He brought the horse into Canada, hired a band, and used savings to buy a tent that could be divided, a portable grandstand, a truck and a semi.

We hit the road as a regular show troupe, with dad, mother

and me leading the procession in the old Buick. The show bill now read: HANK SNOW, 'THE SINGING RANGER,' AND HIS HORSE, SHAWNEE.

We looked for racetracks, fair grounds, or even open fields to hold the show. Then, while mother and I went around nearby towns putting posters in store windows, dad and his band members got ready. They put up the portable grandstand (if one wasn't there already), stationed the flat-bedded truck across from it for a stage platform, strung lights and wiring for the sound system, then stretched the sides of the tent along the ends of the space to cut off outside view.

When we got a crowd and it was dark, the band struck up a fast tune, the spotlight swung to one of the tent wings, and dad came riding in on Shawnee, doffing his hat, and singing a greeting to the audience.

After a few warm-up songs, he executed a series of dare-devil acts. The one that drew the gasps was "the death drag," when he lay across Shawnee's neck and raced the horse back and forth in front of the grandstand.

After intermission came the comedy routines. "How much is two plus two?" he asked. Shawnee tapped four times. "How much is ten divided by two?" The horse tapped five. In answering a straight question, the horse shook his head for no and smiled for yes.

While the band played, dad set two "places" for a "meal" on the ground. Then he sat down on one side and the horse plopped on his haunches opposite and held up his front hooves as if to say, "Pass the potatoes."

The band played softer, the lights dimmed, and the spotlight fell again on dad and the horse. The horse lay down and curled up between its legs. Dad pulled a blanket over both and they pretended to be asleep. Dad pulled at the blanket as if he were cold. The horse grabbed the cover with his mouth and pulled back. The audience loved it.

The lights came on again and dad did rope tricks, standing on Shawnee and spinning the rope over his head, then whirling it around both himself and the horse. At his signal, I came running and jumped up on the stirrup while he kept spinning the rope. We sang a song. I spun the rope a little, then he jumped back on the stage for the finale.

I never saw him drop the rope or miss a cue.

Along the road a juggler named Billy King joined our troupe. I've never seen his match on television or film. He could walk up an unsupported twelve-foot-high ladder, balance on it, and juggle five bowling pins. But his knife act was the most sensational. And I got to be his assistant for it.

Here's how it went: He put a chair on a table and placed a second chair on the first, resting on just two rungs. Then he climbed into the top chair, set a lamp on his head, tucked a big rubber ball in the crook of one knee, balanced another ball on his other foot, and called, "Okay, Jimmie, give me the knives."

I tossed one with the blade open and he flipped it in the air. Two, three, four, five, until he was juggling them all while the audience watched open-mouthed.

But what I liked most about Billy was that he spent time with me. Hours and hours. Listening. Sharing his wisdom. And teaching me to ride a unicycle. He continued riding one to the post office until his death at eighty-two.

A couple of wrestlers traveled with us a few weeks. Before shows I sat and watched them play cards and listened to them discuss who would win that night.

And on occasions we paired up with a carnival. I always had the run of the shows. The Fat Lady. The hootchy-kootchy burlesque acts. Nothing was off limits to me.

We had a few misadventures. Once dad ran the old Buick into a ditch and we turned end over end. But nobody was hurt seriously. Another time the portable grandstand collapsed just before show time. A number of fans were injured.

That fall we returned to West Virginia where we lived in a trailer park next to country singer Hawkshaw Hawkins. I was again enrolled in school, but because of show dates I missed many days. I didn't mind. I figured other kids sitting in dull classrooms should envy me. I was having fun and getting a real education. I was learning that life is a big con game and the object should be to fool as many people as you can for your own pleasure.

But dad and mother weren't happy about my erratic education. When I was eleven dad decided to work out of Moncton, New Brunswick, just above the Maine border, while mother and I lived with a couple of families at different times. I attended fifth grade, went to a Pentecostal Sunday school a few times with one of the mothers and learned how to shoplift in local stores.

All this time dad had been saving money to take Shawnee to Hollywood. If Gene Autry and Roy Rogers had made it in the movies, why couldn't he?

He sent us back to Halifax and left to seek fame and fortune. I was glad to be reunited with my uncles and hoped he'd eventually come back home to stay.

The press agents and con men took him for all he had. All he got was a few pictures with stars and some appearances. He moved on to Dallas where he landed a job singing on KRLD's "Big-D Jamboree" and in a local western-style nightclub.

"Take out papers for permanent residency and join me in Dallas," he wrote and included a money order for train tickets.

I was crushed. What made it harder was that it took several weeks to get the necessary medical exams. I didn't want to leave my uncles, especially Vic. I begged and pleaded to no avail. "Our place is with your father," mother insisted. "We're going."

"You'll meet other friends," she consoled. "And you can write to your uncles."

I was not comforted. I didn't want to make other friends and then have to leave them as had happened so many times before.

All I knew about Texas was cowboys. I didn't see a single one when we reached the station. Lots of men wore wide-brimmed hats. But none swaggered about with sidearms. And the only horse I saw was Shawnee.

Dad didn't have enough money to rent a house. We had to sleep in the truck with the horse.

Our compartment stuck out over the cab and provided barely enough room for the three of us to lie down. To turn over, I had lift myself up.

I slept smack against the front. Then mother and dad with Shawnee in his stall behind us. There was a little sliding door between our compartment and the horse's. Every night he had to have his sugar lumps before he'd let us sleep.

The truck was parked in back of the Roundup Club which fronted on Ervy Street. I soon established a regular routine. I sang with dad for the first show, then danced with perfumed women twice my age or sat around tables with customers until my bedtime. Nobody seemed to care that I was a minor. I just blended into the place.

My friends had always been older people, with the single exception of Uncle Vic. And in Dallas that pattern continued. A steel guitar player, named Butch, was my special friend.

He was a real smoothie with women and had them making offers right in my hearing. "Hey, Butch, how about a little loving after the show?" "I've got to sleep in my big bed all alone. Sure would like some company." I was catching on.

Dad and I sang a few times at the Silver Spur down the street. The big, bull-shouldered owner seemed to like me. I saw him again, fifteen years later. I was watching television coverage of the events immediately following President Kennedy's assassination. The police were escorting Lee Harvey Oswald, the alleged assassin, out of the station for transport elsewhere when, suddenly, a big man in a white cowboy hat lurched out of the crowd and shot Oswald. The big man turned out to be Jack Ruby and, on that day in November 1963, I shuddered to think he had once seemed to like me so well.

I don't want to leave the impression that dad and mother didn't care about my welfare. They did the best they could.

They were concerned about my schooling and insisted I get started right away. Cocky and worldly-wise, I was deflated when they put me, at twelve, into the fifth grade, because of the difference in school systems and my poor attendance in the past. To make matters worse nobody seemed to like me, not because of my strange accent, but because I acted as if I knew everything. I did know a lot more about the seamy side of life than some of the teachers.

The other side of the coin was that I was afraid to get close to anyone. I was sure we'd be moving soon and I didn't want to be hurt again.

Mother gave me a quarter for lunch. What I did was sneak off and go downtown. Bus fare was a nickel, a candy bar five cents, and a movie a dime. That left me five cents to ride home on.

After a few such trips I got tired of having just a candy bar for lunch. I learned how to drop a dime inside a newspaper box and grab change from the shoebox inside along with a paper. I got real good at that.

I cut eighty-six days of school that first year in Dallas and my trusting folks never knew a thing. Why the truant officers didn't contact them, I don't know. Maybe they couldn't find where we lived. After a few months of living in the truck, dad rented a couple of rooms in a rooming house. Then we stayed in a duplex in nearby Urbandale until dad's big chance came nearly two years later.

Dad met Ernest Tubb and discovered they had a common interest in Jimmie Rodgers. Ernest was a big name in country and western and had been on the Grand Ole Opry since 1943. He arranged for dad to make a guest appearance. The Opry management liked dad and he was on.

It was a dream come true. The Opry had been on the air since 1925 and had become the most prestigious of all the country-music radio shows. Members were paid only about forty dollars for an appearance, but the affiliation and the exposure counted in show dates and record sales.

I wasn't excited about moving to Nashville. But I was glad to get out of Dallas. We left just before Christmas, 1949, taking Shawnee along in the truck. As we came into the music city on old U.S. 70, mother remarked that this was one of the dirtiest towns she'd ever seen.

Dad had come up in the world and had rented a small square brick house in the little northern, tree-shaded suburb of Madison. "You'll like it, Jimmie," he assured me. "It sits on a hill, has a nice yard, and there are lots of kids your age in the neighborhood."

There certainly were plenty of kids close by. Our yard adjoined the grounds of the Amqui Elementary School which I would be attending.

I wondered what I had done to deserve this.

4
Lonely Rebel

I was almost fourteen years old and halfway through the sixth grade when we moved to Nashville.

There was no escaping from school here. Mother could see me out the side door and watch through the kitchen window as I crossed the school yard. I could only make the best out of a bad situation.

The first day I took two decks of cards and a pair of dice and set up operations in a corner of the school yard during recess. When I had to stay inside I practiced finger skills by lifting wallets from pockets and purses. At test time I gave kids part of their money back for the privilege of copying from their papers.

I became a whiz at creating trouble in class. I talked out loud, punched my neighbors, and dipped girls' pigtails in ink wells. Three and four times a week I was in the principal's office. She wore out a dozen paddles and switches on me.

My worst whipping came in the eighth grade when Rich Jordan and I were caught learning geography in an unapproved way. We were reading cities aloud off a map, prefacing each name with a degrading adjective that began with the same letter—"Damned Dallas" on so on. Every time the principal swung, my feet left the floor. They could hear me yelling on the other side of the building.

Rich was barrel-chested and had the arms of a weight lifter. I was as skinny as a rail. We got along great because we were so much alike in character. If a kid insulted either of us, Rich would beat him up.

Dad and mother bought a new house, along with some acreage on which the aging Shawnee could graze. Dad's dream was deservedly coming true. His first big hit, "I'm Moving On," was number one on country charts and he was getting top money for shows.

Dad didn't keep up with his money then as well as he does now. I noticed that at night he slipped his wallet between the mattress and box spring. So I set my alarm for about three in the morning. When it rang I turned it off quickly, waited a few minutes to be sure he or mother hadn't heard it, then slipped into their bedroom.

Crawling up to Dad's side of the bed, I listened for his snoring. When assured that he was sound asleep, I eased one hand under the mattress, pulled out the wallet, and extracted a couple of bills. Then I put the wallet back and crawled back to my room. There I flipped on a light and checked the denominations. A hundred and a twenty.

The next day I casually pushed the C-note across the counter to the cashier in the school cafeteria. She picked it up, eyed me suspiciously, and frowned, "Where'd you get this, Jimmie?"

I gave her a superior smirk. "Oh, don't you know my dad is a big Opry star? He gave it to me. Now can I have the change?"

Dad never said anything, so a few nights later I tried it again. I was disappointed to get only a couple of tens. But the next week I got a fifty and a five.

When dad was away for a few days, I snitched from mother's grocery money. I noticed her adding up figures. "Jimmie, I'm missing several dollars. You didn't take anything, did you?"

"Oh, no, I wouldn't without asking," I replied with a stricken look.

"Well, I guess I must have miscounted." And she went on to the store. I didn't try that trick again.

I really didn't need to steal from mother. With what I got from dad plus the money Rich swiped from the till in his father's grocery store, we had plenty to live it up on. After school we had a taxi driver waiting. "See ya," we waved to our classmates boarding the bus, as we strutted to our waiting cab.

"Where to, fellows?" Bert the driver asked respectfully. And off we went for a spin around Nashville.

We were good to Bert and he was good to us. When we asked if he could get us each a pistol, he said, "Sure," and brought a couple of Lugers to school the next afternoon. I carried mine loaded in my book bag, but I was very careful who I let see it.

In all my stupid ways I was trying to impress my peers and make them like me. I failed miserably. Nobody wanted to sit near me in the classroom. Many wouldn't even speak to me. When sides were chosen for a game, I was always selected last—even after Rich.

Dad being on the Opry didn't make many points for me. At that time Opry people weren't very high on the social scale around Nashville. The sophisticates preferred that the city be known as "The Athens of the South" for its educational and publishing institutions and its replica of the Parthenon. The Opry was for country hicks who came from out of town to hear a bunch of honky-tonk musicians play on weekends at the old Ryman Auditorium.

The attitudes of the parents rubbed off on the kids who could care less that I was Hank Snow's son. Nor were they awed by the show tours I made. When I mentioned that I'd just been to Canada and signed 2,000 autographs after one show, their response was, "So what."

But the hardest slap in the face came when the class prophet announced, "Jimmie Snow, most unlikely to succeed."

I didn't expect ninth grade to be any better, and it wasn't. Because the new Madison High School was unfinished, I started in the adjoining town of Goodlettsville. After a couple of months, the principal called me in. "Jimmie, we're at the end of our rope. You skip school, sass teachers, steal, gamble on school premises, and corrupt your classmates." Then fastening a cold stare, he asked, "What do you think can be done to straighten you out?"

Pulling in my lip, I looked at him in feigned contrition. "Sir, I think I could do better if you'd transfer me to another school. I'd make a fresh start."

Glad to be off the hook, he moved me to Isaac Litton High immediately.

I had been pestering dad to buy a motorcycle. "Of course, I know how to ride one," I assured him. "Rich taught me." It was a lie. But he believed me and went down and bought a new Harley-Davidson.

Only the mercy of God kept me alive that winter. I had a half dozen wrecks, the worst occurring when I was roaring down a hill without gloves on a bitterly cold day. While changing hands on the handlebars, I felt my right pants leg catch and took my eyes off the road to look down. Whomp! The front wheel bounced in a hole and I went sailing over the handle bars, landing face first on the concrete and sliding about ten feet. I had to lay in a bed of cotton the next three days.

By this time they were on to me at Isaac Litton and with Madison High now open they transferred me there. When the school year ended, I threw my books on the floor and vowed never to go back.

My folks were disappointed by my decision, but at sixteen I was legally free to drop out. The school officials probably breathed sighs of relief.

The one place where I felt comfortable was at the Opry. The fans' eyes would light up at the name Jimmie Rodgers Snow. And the performers backstage treated me and the other Opry kids like family.

In the early fifties the Opry had around thirty acts, about half the number on the roster now. It didn't matter what the Nashville snobs thought. To me these performers were the greatest people in the world.

Roy Acuff, Ernest Tubb, Minnie Pearl, Red Foley, Hank Williams and all the rest.

I liked to stand in the wings and hear Roy Acuff do his imitation of a train whistle on "The Wabash Cannon Ball." I tapped my feet when Ernest Tubb sang, "I'm Walking the Floor over You." I laughed when Jamup and Honey did their comedy routine and when Minnie Pearl came out swinging her long cotton dress and drawling, "How-dee, I'm jist so glad to be here."

The press agents painted the Opry artists as wholesome, family-loving, God-fearing, just-folks people who lived to make their fans happy. Some were that way, others a little less. And some had more problems than they could manage.

Take Hank Williams. Hank came to the Opry in 1949, a year before dad. When I knew him he was making more money than he could keep track of and was signed to a movie contract with MGM. Hank "lived" a song when he sang it. When he did "Cold, Cold Heart," you felt he had been betrayed by his sweetheart. When he sang, "I Laid My Mother Away," he seemed to be looking at her in the coffin.

Many Opry people drank to relax and break the boredom between shows on the road. But with Hank drinking became an insatiable passion.

It became a challenge to keep him sober. Guys on the road would search his bags, shadow him, eat with him, and lock him in his room until time to leave for the auditorium or theater.

When they'd come to get him, he'd be drunk as a skunk.

They couldn't figure out where he was getting the booze until somebody opened a shaving tonic bottle. He had filled it, a cologne bottle, and several pill bottles with whiskey.

I heard other stories about Hank, but I only know that he was nice to me. Whenever he came off stage, he always bent down to exchange a few words. He was so tall, I had to look up at him, way up. I felt he cared for me personally, not just because I was Hank Snow's son.

Red Foley was another favorite of mine. I don't know of anybody who didn't like this red-haired singer. He'd stand for hours and sign autographs for every kid in line.

When Red sang "Peace in the Valley" and "Just a Closer Walk with Thee" you could see tears in his eyes. Those of us who knew him never doubted his sincerity.

The tragedy was that Red couldn't be what he wanted. He often vowed to quit drinking and serve God. He talked about becoming a preacher. But he always fell back. He admitted that he was his own worst enemy.

Red's marital life was darkened by sadness. His wife died giving birth to their first child. His second wife, a beautiful former showgirl who bore him three daughters, committed suicide after hearing that Red was involved with a Nashville nightclub singer. Red married the singer but didn't find lasting happiness and died an unhappy man in 1952.

Such stories about Red Foley, Hank Williams, and a few others around the Opry, didn't sway me. As a young teenager, I couldn't see myself ending up this way. After all, I didn't drink or take drugs.

Away from the Opry, I was still trying to make it with my peer group. At that time the hangout for younger teens in Madison was at the corner of Old Hickory and Gallatin Road. Here a local group showed free movies on Saturday afternoons for kids. I never missed.

One cool October day I was introduced to a pretty, dark-eyed girl with long brown hair. When Joyce Harrod looked at me I melted and couldn't think of anything to say.

The next Saturday she let me walk her home and after a few weeks her parents invited me to supper.

I was diving into the meat loaf when her dad cleared his throat. I looked around and saw their heads were bowed.

After the meal Joyce's mother asked, "Do you know the Lord, Jimmie?"

"Oh, sure," I mumbled. "I know Him." I figured if I didn't, He ought to know me. I had used His name often enough in conversation. Not around Joyce and her folks of course.

I was sixteen and Joyce had just turned fourteen. Certainly, I thought, we were old enough to go to a regular movie theater together. Her mother said no. "But you can take her to church," she consented.

I was so smitten I was willing to do even that. I sat a few pews back of the Harrods, as close to Joyce as I dared. The singing didn't touch me. I knew country entertainers who sang some of the same songs on the stage, then went out afterwards and got drunk. It was the preaching and the call for sinners to come forward and get saved from sin that got to me.

I had lied, cheated, and stolen from just about everybody except the Harrods. That was me, Jimmie Rodgers Snow, a sinner. A big sinner. If there was a hell for sinners I would probably go there.

I tried to think more pleasant thoughts about Joyce, motor-cycles, the Opry. Still, something kept gnawing, tugging, reminding, "Jimmie Snow, you can con every person on earth, but you can't con God. He knows all about you."

The preacher was sweating and shouting. "Give God a chance. Let Him wash your sins away. Come tonight. Come. Come."

My knuckles were white. I twisted and looked around.

There was no way to get out without Joyce and her folks knowing.

"Tonight may be your last chance. Come on. Come on."

The choir was singing,

Just as I am without one plea,
But that thy blood was shed for me,
And that thou bid'st me come to Thee,
O Lamb of God, I come, I come.

People were crying all around me. I saw a woman walk forward and fall at the front. "Oh, Jesus, help me! Forgive me! Mercy, Jesus. Mercy," she begged. My chest was pounding.

JIMMIE SNOW, WHAT IF YOU WERE TO DIE TONIGHT?

JIMMIE SNOW, WHAT WILL YOU SAY WHEN YOU STAND BEFORE GOD?

JIMMIE SNOW, YOU ARE GOING TO HELL.

JIMMIE SNOW, JESUS LOVES YOU. JESUS LOVES YOU.

"Yes, Jesus loves me. Yes, Jesus loves me." The first song I had ever sung in public.

"Jesus loves me. No matter what I've done. Yes, Jesus loves me!"

I felt an arm about me. It was a boy I had gone to school with, George Hipe, Jr. "Wouldn't you like to go to the altar and turn it all over to Jesus?" he asked gently.

I felt panicky. Closed in by the crowd. The only way to escape would be to follow him out to the aisle and then turn to the right and dash out of there. I had to get away.

I followed him, but when I reached the aisle I realized my feet had taken me to the left and I was headed for the altar. But more important, I was headed toward Jesus, the only one who could forgive me of all my sin.

"It's Hank Snow's son," I heard the whisper repeated over and over as I made my way to the front. But it didn't matter. All I could think of was Jesus.

It seemed such a long way to the altar, but when we finally

arrived my friend knelt beside me and began quoting Scriptures about how God's Son, Jesus, had died on the cross for my sins. "He's knocking on your heart's door, Jimmie. Ask Him to come in."

"Jesus, come into my heart," I prayed. "I know you died for me."

"Praise the Lord! Praise the Lord!" Others were around me shouting. I didn't really know what was happening. I just felt different and clean all over.

When I got home, mother asked where I'd been.

"To church with Joyce," was all I said.

Joyce and I lasted until spring. I was too possessive. Every time she spoke to another boy, I got jealous. We broke up and went back together. Then we drifted apart.

I was now driving. Dad had made the down payment on a '51 Pontiac. "You have to make the payments," he insisted.

My only income was from occasional show tours with dad and a small allowance. I was tired of being dad's protege. If I continued, I wanted to be my own person and dress and sing as I pleased.

"No thanks, I'd rather stay home," I told him.

It was either let the car go back or take a regular job. I applied to the Tennessee Highway Department and was put in a work crew. My main responsibility was scraping up dead dogs and cats along the highway.

The next Sunday morning I stayed in bed. With no romantic interest, I had no desire to get up and dress for church. There was also the distasteful prospect of kidding by my crewmates.

I was the youngest of the group, pimple-faced and scrawny, ready-made for ribbing.

"Hey, Snow, have a swig of muscatel."

"Nah, I wouldn't care for it."

"Oh, come on, boy. Ain't you man enough for a little wine? It won't make you puke."

The others guffawed. I shook my head and stalked off.

I was remembering how dad would lay it on me twice as hard when he was drinking. I had never liked him drunk, except when he came home with a lot of money. And I had seen what drinking could do to others.

They kept it up. "C'mon, Snow, you still a baby?" "It ain't gonna poison you." "Whatsa matter, don't you like us?"

I didn't want to be a loner. I desperately wanted to be accepted. I picked up a jug and guzzled. The liquid tingled my throat. I liked it. I took another swig. And another.

I quit the highway crew in the fall. There had to be a better way to make the car payments than scraping up dead animals. I decided to try show business again.

The month before, Hank Williams had been fired from the Opry for drunkenness and irresponsibility. He had divorced his wife, Audrey, married again, and gone back to Louisiana. According to the grapevine, he was taking prescription drugs to ease the pain of a spinal ailment and was in bad shape.

The following New Year's night Hank was riding in the back of a Cadillac on his way to keep a holiday show date in Canton, Ohio, when he collapsed and died of a fatal heart attack. He was only twenty-nine.

I felt sorry for Hank, his ex-wife Audrey, his surviving wife and his kids. But I told myself, "It'll never happen to me."

5
Prodigal Son

A new opportunity opened when dad and Colonel Tom Parker formed Jamboree Attractions and began lining up talent for show tours. They signed up Mother Maybelle and the Carter Sisters, the Duke of Paducah, Faron Young, Marty Robbins, and a number of new personalities. One of the new talents was a lanky, drawling hillbilly type who did a monologue of a country boy viewing his first football game. Andy Griffith.

I joined this group, not as Hank Snow's son, but as Jimmie Rodgers Snow. It looked like my big chance, for Tom Parker was the best manager and promoter in the business.

This old cigar-chomping gent was already a living legend. Where two or three entertainers got together, you could always count on a Colonel Parker story.

He was better than anyone else at squeezing every dollar out of a show tour. One way he did this was to use one cast for shows in two towns, as much as a hundred miles apart, the same night. He'd start the show in the first town about seven in the evening. The first performers would do their thing, then race to the second town, and be on stage by 8:30. The others would follow as they finished their acts. He ran the artists ragged, but he doubled their money.

Tom had just split with Eddy Arnold before joining up with dad. Because Eddy was popular at rodeos and livestock shows, Tom carried along a box of chickens marked "Livestock Exhibit" to keep from paying a twenty-dollar entertainment tax. When Eddy got sick, Tom slipped a two-dollar hotplate under the chicken cage and billed it as a substitute act called "Colonel Parker's Dancing Chickens." When the Texas Plowboys played "Turkey in the Straw" the audience saw the poor chickens dancing around the cage, trying to avoid the hotfoot. It's a wonder he wasn't cited by the S.P.C.A.

Tom had a peculiar sense for sizing up star potential. When he spotted someone he thought would be a winner, he began working to bring him under his managerial umbrella.

At the time he began working with dad he had his eye on a hip-wiggling Mississippi country boy who was raising dust in Memphis. It didn't matter to Tom that a lot of country music people didn't like him. Tom could smell the box office bacon a 'cookin.'

Dad was hosting a thirty-minute segment of the Opry in 1954. When he said, "Will you welcome Mr. Elvis Presley," the audience saw a young man come on stage with long sideburns and curls hanging jauntily over his forehead. He sang "Blue Moon of Kentucky," a bluegrass number, and "That's All Right" (Mama), a rhythm-and-blues piece. The songs were acceptable, but the hip-wiggling wasn't. Afterwards Opry manager Jim Denny suggested he go back to driving a truck. His biographer says he cried all the way back to Memphis and that he was months getting over the rejection.

Tom had no such scruples. Convinced that Elvis was a future smash, he arranged with the young singer's manager, Memphis deejay Bob Neal, for Elvis to join a Jamboree Attraction tour in the Southwest.

Elvis and his two "Blue Moon Boys" caught up with us in Carlsbad, New Mexico, and worked under Jamboree Attractions until the tour ended in Bastrop, Louisiana, ten days later. His name appeared way down the show bill, even below mine. Then after an unsuccessful tryout with Arthur Godfrey's Talent Scouts in New York, he returned for a three-week sweep with Jamboree through the South, starting in New Orleans May 1 and climaxing in Chattanooga.

"Elvis the Pelvis," as he was already being called, sauntered on stage in black pants with pink stripes down the legs, topped off by a black jacket and pink shirt with collar turned up to catch the ends of his black hair. Guitar hanging from his neck, curls dangling over his forehead, eyebrows arching over lidded eyes, he grinned seductively at the girls in the front rows.

Leaning forward with feet apart and clutching the mike, he warmed up with a slow ballad, then jumped into what the crowd came to see. Hips grinding and shaking, legs jerking and snapping, arms flailing the guitar to a fast drum beat, he drove the females into hysterics.

When Elvis finished, the women ran for him, throwing underwear and keys, and tearing at his clothes. Tom Parker didn't mind, though. He just looked the other way and counted the money.

Tom was a cunning fellow. He knew I wanted to break loose from dad and do my own thing, and that I got along well with Elvis. So he booked me on a separate tour with Elvis. He wanted full control over Elvis and he saw me as a way to bring him into the fold.

Our first show together was in an auditorium in Lubbock, Texas. When we arrived the sponsors had police protection waiting. They said a lot of guys were jealous and had made threats against Elvis. The bodyguards didn't leave us until we were getting in our cars after the last show. Then a fellow, friendly like, called Elvis over. Elvis figured he only wanted an autograph and walked over to the car. The guy reached out and smacked Elvis in the face. Then he raced off. Elvis made us drive around Lubbock until five in the morning looking for him.

Elvis and I made a strange pair. He dressed like a dude, clowned and capered, and was the life of the party. I wore a straight cowboy suit and sat around trying to think of something to say. He didn't smoke, drink, or curse and sirred and ma'amed everybody over twenty-one. I had all the vices and wore a chip on my shoulder. But we both liked girls for sex and boys for company.

He was always loose as a goose and unpredictable. We never knew what to expect next. One night we were riding along and he threw out a band member's shoe. We had to stop the car and go back and find it. Another night we were parked and he tossed away the keys to the car. Whatever he felt like doing, he did, while I was reserved and uptight.

He knew church songs and could quote the Bible like a Sunday school teacher. He claimed to have picked up his body movements from preachers. He always seemed respectful of God. I never heard him take God's name in vain.

As we moved from city to city, the crowds got bigger and noisier. There was always the danger of what jealous boyfriends and husbands might do. But we became more afraid of the females. In Jacksonville, Florida, we had to run for our lives across the football field in the Gator Bowl Stadium. The women were coming after us like a pack of wild wolves, screaming and tearing at our clothes. It was wild, crazy, weird, scary.

By working through people around Elvis, of whom I was only one, Tom Parker finally got Elvis. He had to take on the Memphis deejay as Elvis' "manager." But the card read: Colonel Tom Parker, *General Manager*, Jamboree Attractions.

Later Tom left dad and me to give complete attention to Elvis.

I also worked with Bill Haley and other rock-and-rollers, none of whom had the unique magnetism of Elvis.

Bill gyrated and moved his body sensually, but he didn't have Elvis' wiggle. What he did have was a lot of tricks to send an audience into orbit. For one, the instrumentalists and pianists would stop while the drummer played faster and faster until he busted his stick. Then without losing a beat, he hit the cymbals with his hands until they would bleed. When the crowd saw the blood, they flew into a heathen frenzy.

But Elvis was the pioneer of the rock-and-roll craze. Before he came on the scene, country was country, pop was pop, and rhythm-and-blues was rhythm-and-blues. Elvis ran them all together with a fast beat and set a style which Haley, the Beatles, and others picked up.

I might have made the crossover into rock-and-roll, if I had been able to discipline myself. For a while it was alcohol. Some nights I was so stoned I couldn't even remember going on stage. Then it was alcohol plus pills, the deadly combination that has cut short so many careers in the entertainment world.

The first time I tried pills was in May, 1954, at the second Jimmie Rodgers memorial celebration in Meridian, Mississippi. Dad and Ernest Tubb had started the annual event the year before and this time a whole slew of performers were there, including Elvis, Brenda Lee, Tommy Sands, the Everly Brothers, dad, Ernest, and Hank Thompson.

I'd been drinking and told one of Hank's band members that I couldn't sing that night. He slipped me a couple of speckled Benzedrines. "These'll give you the lift you need," he promised. The pills got to be a regular habit after that.

Benzedrines, Dexedrines, and other "uppers" pulled me out of alcohol depression and kept me awake during a performance. Depressant "downers" such as Seconal and phenobarbital calmed me when I was strung out and tense.

The musicians seemed to have an endless supply. When they ran out, someone picked out a doctor's name from the telephone directory and called for a prescription. Most doctors were pushovers for a performer's line that he had a long drive ahead and needed to stay awake, or that he needed something to go to sleep.

Before a year was up word had gotten around that I was addicted to pills and alcohol. People had had patience with me because I was Hank Snow's son. But I couldn't ride on dad's coattails forever. This became evident as booking dates began dropping off.

I was losing the desire to make it on my own anyway. Alcohol and drugs have a way of dimming ambition.

I was fed up with tours. The long drives between one-night stands. The plastic motel rooms. The impersonal faces. The slick promoters. Elvis and Bill Haley and Tommy Sands could have it.

The squares down at the Opry could have their music, too, I felt. They could please the hamburger-and-root-beer middle class tourists who came from out of town to see them.

I just plain didn't care for anything except bar-hopping, hot-rodding, and picking up women. It wasn't especially exciting. It was just a way to get from one boring day to the next with the least possible pain.

At nineteen my schedule went something like this: Get up around noon and eat. Mess around the house a couple of hours. Then head out for Caldwell's Tavern on Dickerson Road in north Nashville. About seven or eight take in a movie. After the show scout around with a friend looking for girls. Around eleven or twelve stop off at the Greenbriar, a dinky little night club near Tom Parker's office on Gallatin Road. After the Greenbriar closed, maybe go to somebody's house for a party. Or if I had a date I wanted to impress, instead of going to the Greenbriar, run over to the Starlight Club on Dickerson, Big

Jeff's out on the Clarksville Highway, or some classy place in Printer's Alley in downtown Nashville. Some nights I took a woman to a motel, had sex, got her drunk, robbed her while she was still out, and left. Sometimes I stayed drunk two or three days at a time and then, upon arriving home, told my folks I had been on a fishing trip.

One of the few people I felt comfortable with was Suzy Caldwell. When I banged the door of the beer joint, she always had a big smile. "Hi, Jimmie. Good to see you. What'll you have?" If I was broke, Suzy would set me up anyway, then sit and talk until the five o'clock customers came in.

Suzy was twice my age and thin with reddish-brown hair and pretty teeth. Always friendly and ready to listen, she never showboated me among the customers as Hank Snow's son. Same with her husband Harry, when he wasn't loaded.

Suzy and I talked about everything except religion. Often the conversation got raunchy.

"Who'd you make last night, Jimmie?"

"A cute little chick I picked up at the Greenbriar. But I would rather have had you."

I said it in a kidding tone, but given half the chance, I would have gone to bed with Suzy as quickly as with any teenage girl down the street.

Suzy and Harry knew I was under drinking age, but they never had any trouble with the law. When the "wrong" cop came in, Suzy nodded in my direction and I scooted into the back room. The "right" cops paid me no mind.

With all the rough talk, Caldwell's was a friendly place where I saw the same couples day after day. Construction workers, route salesmen, store clerks, and other ordinary working people. Warm and cordial, they didn't put on airs and try to pretend to be what they were not.

One of the few singles who came into Caldwell's was a young guy with curly blond hair named Jerry. We got to be good drinking buddies, except that when he got hung over he always wanted to fight. The drunker I got, the sillier I became.

Jerry pumped gas for his uncle. "Come over and help me out," he invited. "You'll meet some good-looking chicks."

The first afternoon five or six stopped by to tease and flirt with this handsome guy. We took a couple out. They were easy.

Jerry not only got me girls. He also provided a lot of gas for my car and money for drinks.

Jerry and I drifted apart after Burl came on the scene. Burl was fresh from California and a real hep cat—sort of a cross between James Dean and Elvis Presley. He sported a tatooed cross between his right thumb and forefinger. Four little rays ran out from it, each standing for a term in jail. I dug this rakish guy.

I greased my hair and combed curls over my forehead. Just like Burl. But I couldn't smooth talk a girl without getting high on alcohol and pills. Cold sober or high as a kite, Burl was suave and slick. We hung out at the Greenbriar a lot. This was just a dumpy little place with a long bar, a couple of pinball machines, a juke box, two automatic pool tables in front and a dimly-lit room for dancing in back. Police came in but none ever checked my I.D. If they had I was prepared, for I had altered my age on my driver's license.

Sometimes we took girls to the Greenbriar or we went stag and picked up a couple. There were always a few unattached secretaries, store clerks, or housewives hanging around.

After Burl left town I had several male friends, none very close. With a few drinks under my belt, I now felt confident enough to approach a woman on my own.

When I took a date to a classy nightclub, I always made sure I was known to the emcee. He would usually introduce me and announce: "Ladies and gentlemen, we're privileged to have country singer Jimmie Rodgers Snow with us tonight. Jimmie, how about giving us one of your favorites."

After a song the girl thought I was the biggest star in Nashville. And the drinks and dinner were usually on the house.

I seldom dated a girl more than twice. The minute one started to get serious, I dumped her. However, one old friend, a twice-married high school beauty queen, almost got me. We were halfway to Memphis, on our way to get married, when I sobered up enough to turn around and head back home.

I liked another girl even better. She was dark-haired and pretty, very quiet, a year older than I and also twice divorced. I took her all around to the places where I could sing. She was impressed.

One night we went to the Greenbriar and I saw her get high for the first time. She turned into a different person. She jumped on top of the table and started taking off her clothes. Blouse. Skirt. Slip. All the way down to her panties. We all sat there in shock. In the mid-fifties customers just didn't do that in nightclubs in Nashville.

One of the biggest shocks I ever got came when a homosexual cop propositioned me one night outside the Greenbriar. I hit the creep and ran back into the club to warn everybody.

I still went down to the Opry about once a month and did an occasional out-of-town show. But my heart wasn't in the music business.

The one event I did look forward to every year was the fall deejay convention. Everybody in country music was there. Vocalists, pickers, fiddlers, comedians, promoters, writers, recording companies, and all the big deejays. Everybody. Deals were made. Songs pitched. Artists signed. Tour packages put together. Celebrity interviews taped by the deejays for their home folks.

I went to see old friends, drink the free liquor and meet new women. Every recording company had a hospitality suite with an open bar. Girls ran in and out of bedrooms like they were in a brothel. The headquarters hotel turned into Babylon for a week.

"Hey, Jimmie, let's have one for old times' sake." Tommy Sands. "Hey, Jimmie, how about taking me out on the town tonight?" Gene "Blue Suede Shoes" Vincent. "Hey, Jimmie, pour me a big one." Wanda Jackson. Wanda could really put it away then. Now she and her husband are working full-time for God.

By the second day I was totally smashed and stayed that way until the end of the convention.

Wild as I was, mother didn't even know I was drinking. Dad knew and had been shielding her. He had been getting calls warning, "Hank, you'd better do something about Jimmie."

When he tried to talk some sense into me, I'd stomp off and wouldn't come back home for three days.

On one of these layouts two other guys and I got drunk in a motel and nailed all the furniture in the room to the ceiling. Because I had signed the register, the manager sent the police after me. I headed them off in the yard and paid the damages.

"Who was that?" mother asked.

"Just a couple of guys who stopped to say hello. They left."

My lying, conning days were numbered.

Dad intercepted some phone calls from bars where I owed money from buying drinks for my friends. It was just another way of trying to buy popularity.

He looked at me skeptically. "Well, are you going to settle up?"

"Sure," I promised. And I did. Even if I had to steal the money to do it.

Then he got ahold of my driver's license and saw that I had changed my birth date. He blew up, and I took off again.

He tried a new ploy. One night he followed me downtown and watched me go into a club. Parking across the street, he called the manager from a pay booth. "I can see your front door. You've got an under-aged boy in there, and if he isn't out in two minutes, I'm calling the police." Out I went.

I avoided dad as much as possible, staying away when I knew he was home. I kept up a front before mother. Poor trusting soul. A mother is the last person to believe something bad about her kid.

Then came the day when dad dragged me into his office.

"Sit down, I have something to show you." He pointed to his insurance policies and will on the desk. "I want you to know that your name's been taken off."

I looked at the lines where my name had once been and was now missing. I felt numb. "You've disinherited me?"

"Yes. We can't do nothin' with you. But you will always have a place to sleep and eat here. I know how it is to get kicked out. I'd never do that to you." His voice was quieter, softer, older, and resigned.

Without saying a word to mother and dad, I went downtown to the army recruiting office. I was already in the air force reserves, having signed up the year before to avoid being drafted. Now I told the sergeant, "I want to enlist."

He looked at my identification papers. "You were born in Canada, I see."

"Yes sir, but I have permanent residency status. So have my dad and mother. This is our home now."

He asked a few more questions and seemed satisfied. "You'll be hearing from us," he promised.

About five weeks passed. I kept my folks in the dark. Then the notice came. REPORT FOR DUTY, JANUARY SIXTH, 0800.

I began packing secretly. Dad and the establishment could go to hell.

6
Hounds of Heaven

January 3, 1956. Three days before I was to leave for camp. I was down to fifty cents.

"Going to the movies at the Skyway," I yelled to mother. I was still speaking to her.

I backed out of the driveway, not looking to see if a car was coming over the hill behind me, shifted to drive, and squealed the tires of my '54 Olds. North on Marthona three blocks to Old Hickory Blvd. West along Old Hickory, then south on Dickerson.

"Maybelline, why can't you be true? Maybelline . . ." I was tapping my left foot to Chuck Berry's big hit.

". . . why can't you be true?" I slowed to turn left across the median of the four-lane highway.

About a quarter to seven on a cool winter night. My blinker was on. The drive-in was in sight.

Suddenly everything went black.

The next thing I remember was a voice asking, "Where's your driver's license, son?" Then blackness again.

I woke up at the hospital. I couldn't see. They told me later my face was matted with blood. One eyelid cut off. Lips split clear up into my nose. A deep gash in my forehead. My right thigh bone sticking out of the flesh. A big hole in my chest.

They were dry shaving my broken leg for an operation. I was about to come out of the bed when I felt big hands wrench my right leg around to jerk the bone back into the socket.

"Yeowww! Yeowww!"

I felt a big needle jab into my backside. Mercifully, I passed out again.

When I next awoke the room had changed. Sunlight was streaming through a window across from my bed. Mother and dad were sitting close by.

My right foot felt as if somebody were holding a torch to it. I hollered and a nurse came in and administered a pain killer.

"What happened?" I moaned as the drug was taking effect.

Dad gave me the details from the police report.

As I was coming south, slowing to turn left, the drunk had been racing north, fleeing police in a stolen '56 Chevy. They had clocked him at 105 mph just before he hit me head on. He had been brought in with a broken jaw and three or four broken ribs and wasn't seriously injured.

The force of the crash had split the engine of my Olds in two, driving the plastic nub on the steering wheel back into my chest where it shattered, coming within a fraction of smashing my heart. Simultaneously, the steering column had pierced my thigh, driving the bone all the way through. After cutting me out of the car, they found the shoes I had been wearing in the back seat, tied and laced.

A strange woman came into the room. "My husband was the one who hit you," she sobbed. "I've tried to get him to stop drinking. I'm so sorry.

"We have children and a little house. If you press charges and win, you won't get much. But it'll be all we have." She was begging.

Dad and mother assured her we wouldn't sue. It was enough that I was alive.

They announced my accident at the Opry over Radio WSM and invited fans to write get-well letters. The mail came in by the sackful. At ten thousand letters we stopped counting. Fan magazines published pictures of me in the hospital bed almost buried under mail.

Outside of my folks, E. J. and Maybelle Carter, and a few of dad's close friends on the Opry, I didn't have many visitors. Elaine Tubb, Ernest's daughter, came. We were good friends and she was very sympathetic. The girl who did the strip at the Greenbriar came a couple of times. I thanked her but didn't feel any affection for her.

On the tenth day of February, thirty-eight days from the time of the accident, dad and mother brought me home with a sixteen-inch steel pin in my leg. I walked on crutches for several more weeks and used a cane until September.

During that time I did manage to hobble down to the Federal Courthouse building on Broadway with my folks so the three of us could be sworn in as citizens of the United States. That was a proud moment.

But I'd never be able to serve my new country in the army because of the accident. When dad gave them the medical report, they canceled my enlistment and classified me 4-F.

But my mother and dad were grateful to have me alive. Dad put some souvenirs of my survival in a glass case in his private museum at the house: two quarters and a tube of Chapstick I had in my pocket when hit. Both quarters were bloodstained and one had been driven into the tube of balm by the force of impact.

If dad was hoping the wreck would turn me around, he hoped in vain. I was only grudgingly grateful for their care, and only a little thankful to be alive. I still couldn't see much worth living for, except partying and womanizing.

As soon as I could hobble, I fell back into the old routine. I came and went as I pleased. Stayed away from home as long as I wished. Remained drunk for days and afterwards couldn't remember anything I had done.

There was nothing my parents or anyone could do to keep me from destroying myself. I was out-of-control and I didn't have enough will power to step on the brakes.

I still liked music. But I had no ambition to be anybody. Just drinking, carousing, and partying. Living from one day to the next.

Old pals in show business such as Elvis Presley, Tommy Sands, and Bill Haley were hitting the big time now. Elvis' new single "Heartbreak Hotel" was knocking the ceiling out of the charts. He was making all the big TV shows and also being groomed for the movies.

I envied Elvis. Not for his talent and good fortune, but for his staying off alcohol, cigarettes, and pills. Me? I was just a dopehead and a drunk, unfit even for the army.

So I continued to hang around Nashville, living off my folks, mooching drinks and pills, running around with low-class women, taking a few show dates, and latching on to the latest fad in hedonism.

The craze in the summer of 1956 was hypnotism. "Nothing to it," an old Opry performer assured me as we were driving to an engagement. "Watch me at the party tonight after the show."

I sat in a corner all eyes and ears. "Now watch this cigarette lighter, Ruby," he told his unsuspecting victim as he held the lighter high over her head so that she had to roll her eyes way back to see it.

"Now relax. Just relax. Relax. Watch the lighter. You're getting sleepy. Sleepy."

Her eyes closed. "Now, Ruby, you're a dog. A dog. Get down on your knees and bark. You'll like it. Bark."

Zombie-like, she slid off the couch.

"You're a dog, Ruby. A dog. Bark. Bark."

"Woof! Woof! Woof!"

He told her to get back on the couch. She did. He snapped his fingers and she came out of the trance.

I tried it with a girl outside the Greenbriar. I laid her flat on her back in the back seat of my car with her head hanging out one door. She'd been drinking a little and was a pushover for sex. Later I took her back into the club and had her cackle like a chicken. She said she didn't remember a thing afterwards.

I used it on several others. One girl I burned with a cigarette. She didn't even feel it. I told her the mark wouldn't be there when she came to. It wasn't. But I discovered I could only go so far with girls who had strong moral inhibitions against illicit sex.

I now believe the power to hypnotize and control another's mind is demonic. It's dangerous for both the person who does it and the one who surrenders his mind. I don't think even doctors should use hypnotism.

At that time it was only a fancy with some in the Nashville music community, a temporary amusement. We were just playing around and got tired of it.

I was also getting more work. For some unknown reason my show dates and record sales increased that fall. I felt there might be some hope if I could break the hold of booze and drugs.

The October deejay convention opened at the Andrew Jackson Hotel. When I arrived the first day the lobby was jammed with old acquaintances backslapping one another and deejays conducting interviews.

"Jimmie Snow, come over here."

I walked over to talk to the deejay from Texas. We shook hands and he flipped on his recorder. "Folks, this is Jimmie Rodgers Snow, son of the famous Hank Snow. How's your own career going, Jimmie?"

"Great, Bill, nice to see you again back in Nashville." I never had been any good for interviews. I was still the same shy little boy, who when introduced could only say, "Good evening, ladies and gentlemen."

Bill thanked me for the time and I went on to the next deejay. An hour later I was still only halfway across the lobby. Then I spotted some familiar faces from West Virginia. Wilma Lee and Stony Cooper, and their teenage daughter Carol. She looked mighty pretty.

I grabbed Stony by the arm. "Welcome to Nashville. I heard that you folks were coming on the Opry."

Wilma Lee and Stony greeted me like a long lost nephew and asked about my folks. Carol flashed a toothy smile. She was a dark-haired beauty; really stunning. I wanted to see more of her.

"Hey, Jimmie, got a minute?" Another deejay.

"See you folks around. If there's anything I can do to help you get settled, let me know." I strode off like a big shot, conscious that Carol's eyes were following.

I had a reason now to go to the Opry when I wasn't guesting. Carol was there with her folks every Saturday night and within a month, we were good friends.

Carol attracted me because she was young and pretty and innocent, the sweet protected fifteen-year-old daughter of two devoutly religious people who really lived up to their press image.

I figured Wilma Lee and Stony had to learn about my reputation, since my activities had long been the scuttle-butt of Nashville gossips. But while they didn't say anything, they hardly let Carol out of their sight. After the Opry, they took her straight home.

They bought a house about ten minutes' drive from my folks. I kept finding excuses to go over. When I couldn't see Carol, I went back to my old haunts to pass the time. I knew I should leave the pills and liquor alone, but the habit was too strong. I went on another binge and didn't get home for three days.

In the spring of '57 dad headed up a twenty-day tour across Canada. Being old friends, it was natural that he ask the Coopers to come along. When I learned Carol was going, all the girls in Nashville couldn't keep me home.

Because we were the only singles on the tour, we were able to spend a lot of time together. I told her I had done a few things I was ashamed of, but intended to stay on track career-wise from now on.

I recalled my experience in the Assembly of God church. "You know, I was really happy there for a while. Really happy. Then I got in with the wrong crowd. I'd sure like to get back to God," I sighed.

"Why don't you?"

"I don't know if I'm ready—or if God will take me back."

I looked at her. She was so intense. So concerned. Abruptly I asked, "Are you saved?"

"I believe in God. And I try to live right."

"That isn't enough, Carol. You've got to see yourself as a sinner and ask God to save you. Believe that Christ died for you. Then start living for Him." I shocked myself. After five years, I still knew what being a Christian was all about.

Yet I was really mixed up. When I talked with Carol I talked about God and a career in show business. When away, I honky-tonked and guzzled whiskey and popped pills. I never drank around her.

RCA Victor signed me to a new recording contract. I did more guesting on the Opry. I knew dad was hoping I'd become a regular member of the elite Opry cast, just as Justin Tubb had followed his father two years before.

Suddenly everything began to click. Governor Frank Clement, who owed me favors for campaign appearances, recommended me to the famous Elia Kazan, the dramatics master who had tutored James Dean. The governor's letter said in part: "His reputation is above reproach and he typifies clean living and good character." What a scream.

Lawrence Welk invited me to appear on his national TV show. Since I would be coming to California, Johnny Bond, an old cowboy actor-singer friend of dad's, set up an appearance on Hollywood's "Townhouse Party" with Tex Ritter and Jimmy Wakely, and several other TV shows. I would be one of the first country artists to be showcased in Hollywood. Elvis Presley, who had come before, could not properly be called country.

Merle Travis, the great guitar picker and author of "Sixteen Tons" and many other songs, picked me up at the L.A. airport. The next two weeks were an exciting melange of appearances, parties, and greeting old friends and making new ones. I talked to Tommy Sands, now married to Nancy Sinatra, and other old acquaintances. But the big moment came when Lawrence Welk said, "Ladies and gentlemen, here from Nashville is a new talent I think you'll like—Mr. Jimmie Rodgers Snow."

I sang "A Fallen Star" and "I'm Saving My Money to Buy You a Rainbow." The studio applause was flattering and I was awed when Lawrence said an estimated seventy million viewers had seen me.

It was a big, big high. I flew home with high ambitions.

Anxious to tell Carol all about my adventures, I hurried over to the Coopers. Wilma Lee and Stony spoiled our reunion by refusing to let us go out. So we sat in their living room and talked. Then I went out and got drunk.

The next day I tossed some mints on my breath and went back. I asked if I could take her to the Assembly of God Church in Madison. Her parents relented and said it would be okay.

A week or so later they agreed I could take her and a girlfriend to see *The Ten Commandments*. I was captivated by the miracles. All the way through I talked to them about God.

The church had a midweek service on Thursday evening. I

asked Stony and Wilma Lee if Carol could go with me again. They said she could.

When the altar call was given for sinners, I urged her to go. She walked down the aisle and knelt at the same spot where I had asked for forgiveness five years before.

When we left the church, her face was shining. I was touched and torn, stricken with guilt and afraid to do anything. I had failed before and I didn't want to fail again.

The next day I scanned the movie columns. *The Ten Commandments* was still on. I went back by myself and sat transfixed when Moses came down from the mount, his face aglow because he had seen God. I wanted more than anything else in this world to have a relationship with God, to be delivered from liquor and drugs and lust, to live pure and clean.

I saw *The Ten Commandments* at least seven times and *Samson and Delilah* twice. After each occasion, I came home and read from the Old Testament to see if the script was following the book.

Late one evening I sat in my bedroom with my Bible open and my heart pounding. I had had an experience with God and had turned back. I knew how to be saved. Yet I had broken every commandment except the sixth. If there was a judgment, and my conscience assured me there was, I was doomed.

There was no way I could con God.

I wanted to throw myself upon His mercy. Yet I was afraid. Afraid that if I did get saved, really get saved, I would have to preach.

Jimmie Rodgers Snow, booze-hound, pillhead, and skirt chaser, a preacher! Impossible. Incredible.

Carol and I talked about getting married. "What would you think of being a preacher's wife?" I ventured.

"If that's what you want, it's all right with me," she said.

I told her goodnight and drove to one of my joints. At three, maybe four in the morning I drove home, so drunk I could have killed somebody.

That's the way it went through the first two weeks of November. Telling Carol I might become a preacher. Then going out and getting drunk.

On the third Saturday night of the month I was backstage at the Opry when Elvis Presley made a walk-on appearance. He still couldn't win a popularity contest at the Opry, but they couldn't ignore him now.

He greeted me in his dressing room like a long lost brother. I introduced him to Carol and a press photographer snapped the three of us arm in arm

"Whatcha doin' in January?" he asked.

"Nuthin' much," I shrugged. "Whatcha got in mind?"

"Come up and spend a couple of weeks with me."

"Sure," I promised. "I'll do that."

I took Carol home. On the way back to my house I stopped off for a few beers.

Drunk again. And every night that week. I couldn't help myself. I couldn't stop. Drinking and then popping pills. Every night. The fourth week in November was so fuzzy I'll never be able to remember all of it.

Then came that fateful Wednesday night, the 27th. I was disgusted with myself beyond understanding. I wanted to marry Carol. I wanted to be a star. I wanted to have my mountain of guilt lifted and be right with God. I wanted to be a preacher and turn people to the light. I wanted the impossible dream.

I couldn't make it to the dawn. I lifted the gun to my mouth, then put it down.

That's when I gave up struggling.

I staggered outside and threw myself upon the mercy of God there by the mailbox.

My life was transformed.

7
Valley of Decision

The first three people I told about my call to the ministry all reacted differently.

Mother thought I was close to having a nervous breakdown.

Carol, starry-eyed at fifteen, didn't feel strongly one way or the other. If that was what I felt God wanted, then it was okay with her.

Pastor Alford encouraged me to get active in the church and make plans to start back to school the next fall. He suggested I apply to Central Bible College (Assemblies of God) in Springfield, Missouri. If I couldn't pass a high school equivalency test, I could take make-up courses there. I told him I would pray and think it over.

As Christmas approached, the aura of the dramatic experience at the mailbox began wearing off. I knew I was saved and forgiven. I had a deep desire to live for God. But I rationalized that my life might count for more in show business.

And there was the promise to spend a couple of weeks with Elvis.

I flew to Memphis on the afternoon of New Year's Day, 1958. Elvis had a Cadillac waiting at the airport.

It was dark when the driver parked before Elvis' big white colonial Graceland Mansion.

Elvis was standing just outside the front door, signing for a special delivery package. "Hiya, Jimmy," he called. "Come in and meet my friends."

I followed him inside the huge two-story mansion. He tossed the package carelessly on a couch and began introducing me to about a dozen other young people gathered around the piano in the living room. Later he casually mentioned that the special delivery was a gold record from RCA. His twenty-third. Nothing to get excited about.

"Let's go eat," Elvis announced, and we all piled into two Caddies. Twenty minutes later we were in the banquet room of a downtown restaurant, feasting on steak and lobster.

We sat around the tables a long time, joking, laughing, having a good time. Then Elvis said, "Let's go skating." He had rented the rink with all its employees.

Same with a theater where we arrived about one thirty in the morning. The movie was his newest release, "Jailhouse Rock." Elvis played the male lead, an ex-con named Vince Everett.

While Elvis hadn't been in prison, there were some obvious parallels. After becoming an overnight sensation in rock music, Vince took Hollywood by storm. And like Elvis, he had an entourage of young friends.

Elvis sat next to me. "What'd ya think of me in that scene?" he asked. "How'd I do?" And, "Was I flat on that note? Did I hold it too long?" All through the film he kept asking for opinions. Towards the end he remarked that during a dance act in the production he had swallowed a porcelain cap from a front tooth and had to have it removed at Cedars of Lebanon Hospital.

Around three thirty we left the theater to drive around Memphis. I was riding in the lead car with Elvis along a four-lane avenue when he shouted to the driver, "Hey, stop it right here." The driver hit the brakes in the middle of the block. Elvis jumped out and began waving his hands at the traffic piling up behind us.

When an impatient driver honked he stuck his tongue out in mockery. He was still the same old impulsive Elvis who did whatever he felt like doing.

When we finally swung back toward Graceland for breakfast, the morning rush hour was starting.

That was the style for the next ten days. Sleep all day and howl all night. Some nights before going out, we sang around the piano, acted silly, and told jokes. Just good, clean fun. There was no playing around; if some of the boys and girls slept together, they did it very privately. Nor did I see anyone drinking.

Elvis' nocturnal habits were understandable. He couldn't go anywhere in the daytime without being mobbed.

"How about goin' to California with me?" he invited. "I'll set you up with some people who can help your career."

It was tempting. If I hadn't wanted to get back to Carol so badly, I might have gone and my future might have turned out differently. As I flew back to Nashville, I felt only one regret: I hadn't told Elvis about what happened at the mailbox.

When I went to Carol's house, I could tell her folks weren't happy to see me. I knew they felt Carol was too young to be romantically involved; that I was too old for her; that my future was too unpredictable; that I wasn't the type they wanted for a son-in-law, even if I was in show business. But all they could do was keep a tight rein on Carol and hope her affections would cool.

I can understand how they felt now. I wouldn't want a twenty-two-year-old fellow with a reputation for drinking and womanizing messing around with my fifteen-year-old daughter either.

I couldn't see it their way then at all. Carol and I were in

love. Sure, I had had a lot of cheap affairs. But God had forgiven
me and had given me Carol, the loveliest, sweetest girl in the
world. What was so wrong for us to love one another and get
married?

Young people in love have a way of not thinking logically, of
not considering the feelings of parents, and even when they are
Christians of taking actions they know are wrong. I'm not
justifying what we did. I'm only saying we followed our hearts
immaturely.

We went downtown and Carol lied about her age to get blood
tests and a marriage license. Then on March 28, 1958, only
seven days after her sixteenth birthday, I picked her up after
school and we drove to Columbia, Tennessee, with a couple of
friends for witnesses and persuaded a Baptist preacher to
marry us. I dropped her back at her house at the time she
customarily got off the school bus.

Two weeks later her folks found out. They were furious and
wanted to get the marriage annulled.

My parents didn't like it either, but said we could live with
them until we found a place. Dad would introduce us at the
Opry as newlyweds. No more sneaking around.

Even after the commotion around our surprise marriage
finally calmed down, I was acutely conscious of my shortcom-
ings. I had failed to share my faith with Elvis Presley. I had
made Carol's folks terribly unhappy. I had led my young
sweetheart to lie about her age on the marriage certificate.
While I had not taken a drink since the holidays I had been
unable to quit smoking. Without booze or pills I couldn't
overcome my shyness; a necessity if I was to become a preacher
or successful entertainer. I was so shy I purposely got to church
late, just so the pastor wouldn't ask me to say something.

I puzzled over a sermon on the baptism of the Holy Spirit.
Pastor Alford said it was an infilling of God, an empowering of
the believer to live a victorious Christian life. "If you're saved,

you have the Spirit living within you," he declared. "If you're filled, the Spirit is in control."

I saw people going to the altar to ask for the baptism. I heard shouts, "Praise God! I'm filled with the Spirit! Glory! Glory!"

Fanaticism, I thought. Too far out for me.

The church had two young preachers in for a revival. Carol and I went. One of the preachers was giving the invitation, when I saw her move out. She was saved already. What was this for? Then I realized she was going for the baptism of the Holy Spirit.

After that she was a different person. Radiant, bubbly, joyful. She talked about the Lord all the way home.

I wanted what she had, but I was still afraid of the fanaticism. I just couldn't let go.

Then one night at the church I was praying with another fellow when, wow! Something hit me in the chest. I fell across the floor, alternately laughing and crying and praising God. I was there three hours; it seemed like ten minutes.

I couldn't explain what had happened. I just knew there was a greater will power in me. I threw away my cigarettes and never smoked again. I talked excitedly about the goodness of God. I couldn't praise Him enough.

Before I had been crying out as Paul did in Romans 7:24: "O wretched man that I am! who shall deliver me from the body of this death?" Now I was in Romans 8, where Paul declared in verse two, "For the law of the Spirit of life in Christ Jesus hath made me free from the law of sin and death."

Paul had written to the Ephesian Christians: "Be not drunk with wine, wherein is excess; but be filled with the Spirit (5:18)." The analogy was so obvious in my case. Once it had taken alcohol to loosen me up. Now it was as if I were drinking again. Drunk with the Spirit. I had changed from an introvert to an extrovert.

But being filled with the Spirit didn't turn me into a robot. I still had to seek the will of God about whether to prepare for the ministry or to stay in show business.

I thought the answer might come during a forty-day tour Carol and I took with dad, the Carter Family, and several other Opry artists. Just before Carol and I sang, I tried to give a brief testimony. The audiences listened respectfully, but some in the tour group weren't overjoyed. They kidded us and told dirty jokes in our presence. One night we were praying aloud in our hotel room when a guitar picker came andcomplained we were making a disturbance. He didn't mention the noisy beer party going on next door.

Carol continued to leave the burden of decision with me. I agonized in prayer for direction. "Lord, you've given me this talent. I can testify before thousands if I stay in show business. It'll take me years to train for the ministry. Please show me the way to go."

My father had made all the decisions concerning my career. He had always told me what to sing and how. Which suit to wear. How to walk and stand. Everything. Now I had to make this momentous decision on my own.

Then one night I walked out on a stage in Toronto and to my surprise, announced, "Folks, this will probably be the last time you'll ever see me appear as an entertainer, because I may go into the ministry." Was God trying to tell me something?

When we got back to Nashville, Pastor Alford invited me to preach the next Sunday evening. "What will I preach about?" I wondered aloud.

"The Lord will give you a message," he assured.

Two days passed and no message. I read a few chapters from my Bible. No theme crystallized in my mind. I thumbed through a little booklet called "Twelve Men and a Light" which someone had given me. On the first page was a picture of an apostle with a brief sketch of his life, on the second page another apostle and something about him, and so on until the final page showed a picture of the twelve apostles with Jesus bathed in light. I could talk briefly about each apostle and wrap up with the thought that while all had different ways of serving God, all followed Jesus as the light.

I asked dad if he'd listen to me rehearse. He nodded his assent and asked me into his office. Actually, I had a second purpose in mind. I wanted to testify to him.

I stood behind a big cowhide reclining chair and spoke about ten minutes. "Sounds good," he pronounced without giving any indication of his personal feelings.

The church liked it too.

But I still had doubts about the wisdom of a career in the ministry. I worried about meeting financial obligations.

Dad and mother had given us a lot adjacent to their home to build on. But we couldn't afford a house and had purchased a house trailer on time payments. Because of the zoning in my folks' neighborhood, we were living in a trailer park about five minutes away.

With both trailer and car payments plus living expenses, I couldn't see how I could go to school. Carol and I were pretty successful in show business now. Why leave security? Why not be a witness on the stage, where I would have enough money to retire in a few years? Then I could preach.

On the other hand: Hadn't God promised to provide? Look what He'd done for me already.

I prayed and debated. Debated and prayed. One night I was calling on the Lord so loudly and earnestly, that a gruff voice yelled from a neighboring trailer, "Shut up and go to sleep!"

Finally I said, "Okay, Lord, if you want me to preach, get me an invitation outside the Madison church by the first of September." I reached up and circled the date on a wall calendar and had peace.

This was August. We did a two-week tour and had just returned when a lady from the church called. "Haven't seen you all in services recently," she said, "and was wondering how you're getting along."

"Yeah, we're fine. We've been on the road."

"Yes, well, uh, I did have another reason for calling. I've been doing a little mission work in a trailer park downtown. God kinda laid it on my heart to ask if you'd help out in a service. You and Carol sing and then you, Jimmy, give your testimony."

"Sure," I agreed without thinking.

"Good, good, I'll expect you. Friday night about eight. On Second Avenue near the Opry House. You can easily find it."

After hanging up, I glanced at the calendar. It was September 1.

A couple of weeks later we were at the trailer park with our guitars. Carol knew quite a few gospel songs and did most of the singing. I knew only "Jesus Loves Me," "The Last Mile of the Way," and "He'll Understand and Say Well Done."

I counted the people in the folding chairs before us. Twenty-two. I stood facing the traffic. To my right was the Ryman where people were lined up for the Opry. I thought of the crowds I had sung before there and the few here. It didn't make sense that I should be a preacher.

A fear seized me: "What if some of the Opry performers come by and recognize me? They'll think I'm really stupid."

I went ahead with my life story, all the time keeping one eye on the sidewalk, hoping no one from the Opry would walk by and recognize me. No one did. If I had made a complete commitment to preach I wouldn't have been ashamed.

I couldn't go all the way and give up show business. The path to the ministry seemed too uncertain and risky. That Carol was looking so trustfully to me made it all the more difficult.

In October our church had another revival. The preacher was Glen Miller, a strapping, dark-haired man from Savannah, Georgia. One night he was preaching about cutting loose from human security and leaning wholly on God. My mind was pitching about on the horns of the dilemma: Show business or the ministry? Which way to go?

"Jimmy and Carol Snow?"

I jumped when the preacher called our names.

"The Lord has given me a word of knowledge for you. He wants you to step out on faith and trust Him."

We held up our hands in acquiescence. "Yes, Lord, we will trust you," I breathed. "Yes, yes, yes." Beside me Carol was voicing her own commitment.

That was the turning point. I canceled all the show dates I could and declined to sign any new commitments. I went to the Baptist Book Store in Nashville and bought a *Thompson Chain-Reference Bible* which Miller recommended. Day after day I sat in the trailer and studied Scripture. Carol continued singing and brought in enough money for us to live on.

Pastor Alford came by. "I'm preaching a revival in a little church on Trinity Lane. Would you fill in when I must come back to our church for services starting next Thursday night?"

I took his request as a command from God.

This time I was determined to prepare my own sermon. Taking as my text Jesus' promise in Luke 24:49 of the enduing of power upon His disciples, I looked up every reference I could find about the Holy Spirit. I stayed up most of one night typing out with one finger four pages of notes.

Thursday night I faced about twenty-five people in the small church. My mother and Maybelle Carter were in the audience.

I laid my notes on the pulpit and began. Four minutes later I was at the bottom of the last page. I was so embarrassed. I had lost my place and didn't know how to go back and pick up the line of thought. Mother didn't help when she remarked afterwards, "I warned you, I'd make you nervous if I came."

I tried to beg off for Sunday night, but Pastor Alford insisted he couldn't get anyone else.

I saw in the paper where an evangelist was preaching at a church across town and I went to hear him Friday night. Sitting near the front, I watched every mannerism and took notes on his sermon. Saturday night I went back and watched him again.

Sunday night I bounced confidently into the pulpit, arranged my notes, mopped my forehead with a white handkerchief as I had seen the evangelist do, cleared my throat, and began reading the text. I was about three minutes into the sermon when the anointing hit me. I shouted and jumped a foot off the floor. Forgetting the canned sermon, I began exhorting. Three people got saved that night. I was so excited I couldn't sleep. I knew then, positively, absolutely, that God wanted me to be a preacher.

There was one more show tour I had to make, a fifteen-day stretch across the Midwest with dad. When we got back, I went to the Baptist Book Store and bought a children's *Hurlburt's Bible Storybook* and began memorizing biographies of Bible characters.

One afternoon in November the phone rang. The caller identified himself as pastor of the Assembly of God in Gallatin, Tennessee. "Jay Alford told me about you," he said. "I'd like to invite you to preach a week's revival starting January third."

The second anniversary of my wreck. I felt tingly all over. "Yes, sir, I'll be there."

I went to work outlining ten sermons, two for each of the Sundays and six for week nights. I ran references, pored over stories in the Hurlburt book, and practiced on Carol.

One night I went to hear another evangelist. What a spellbinder. He was good. Really good. When he gave the invitation people crowded the altar.

I met him and learned he was an ex-performer. We hit it off immediately. He volunteered to come to the trailer and help with my sermon preparation.

"You should have from three to seven main heads that hang

around your main subject," he advised. "Each head should begin with the same letter for easy memory. That's called alliteration. Take the story of the prodigal son. He *rebelled* against his father. He *ran* away from home. He was *ruined* by riotous living. He *repented* of his sin. He *returned* home. He was *reconciled* to his father. There you have *rebelled, ran, ruined, repented, returned,* and *reconciled.* You can preach that without looking at notes and your audience will remember."

I smiled and nodded gratefully.

After a few times together the evangelist proposed that he and his wife and Carol and I form an evangelistic team and travel together.

"We'll have our own tour bus," he promised. "The Lord will use our talents to win thousands."

"Praise the Lord!" I exclaimed. "Isn't that marvelous, Carol? And we were wondering how we'd make it."

Carol smiled her concurrence.

I called Pastor Alford and gave him the good news. He didn't sound thrilled.

A few days later he called me back. "Jimmy, would you go over and talk with our district superintendent? He has some things to discuss with you."

I hurried to the Assemblies of God district office located in north Nashville.

The superintendent gave me a fatherly clap on the shoulder and told me to sit down and be comfortable. "What I have to say won't be very pleasant, Jimmy. But Brother Alford and I have talked it over, and we feel we should talk to you now before you get too involved with this man."

He pushed over a stack of reports. "When we heard you were thinking of going in with him, we did a little checking. It's all here. Records of where he lied and cheated and left debts unpaid across the country."

My eyes burned as I looked through the papers.

"You'll have to pray and make your own decision, son."

"Yes, sir," I mumbled with a constriction in my throat. "Thank you. I'd better get home. Goodbye."

I cried all the way. I had looked upon the evangelist as a spiritual father and now he was proven to be a phony.

Carol was away when I got back to the trailer. I ran inside and grabbed the reference Bible. The tears had dried on my face but the anger and hurt still burned within me.

I stepped outside and hurled the expensive Bible as far as I could. I was sure I wouldn't be needing it any more.

8
The Sawdust Trail

The pastor from Gallatin was on the phone. "Our folks are really looking forward to hearing you, Jimmy. We've got stories in the newspapers and posters all over town. We're expecting capacity—"

"Something has come up," I broke in. "I can't come."

"Huh?"

"I can't make it."

"Oh, I understand your problem. You're a young preacher and scared. Son, you don't have a thing to worry about. We've been praying every night. The Lord will help you."

"I appreciate that, but you'll just have to get someone else."

His voice firmed. "Look, Jimmy, our church took you at your word. We've gone to a lot of trouble publicizing and preparing. You can't pull out now and leave us holding the bag."

The show-must-go-on instinct within me responded. "Okay, I'll speak for you Sunday, but that's all."

Cold hearted and feeling nothing, I waded through the weeds outside the trailer and retrieved the Bible from a ditch. Fortunately the weather had been dry and the book was only dusty and a little soggy from dew. I carried it back in the trailer

71

and began looking up Scriptures. It was just like preparing for a show.

Sunday morning the church was crowded. Carol and I sang. I read my text and told a Bible story memorized from the Hurlburt book. The bitterness faded and I felt the same warmth and unction I had experienced in the little church on Trinity Lane.

"I was the biggest drunk and pillhead you ever saw," I thundered. "I wanted to quit and couldn't. God allowed me to almost die in a car wreck. Still I was unable to break the bonds of sin. I tried to kill myself and failed at that. Then I threw myself on God's mercy. Glory to God, He forgave my sins and gave me peace as I knelt that cold winter night by the mailbox. Praise God for His mercy! Praise Him for His salvation! Praise Him for His Holy Spirit!! Hallelujah!!"

My coat and tie were off, my sleeves rolled up. I was perspiring and pacing back and forth in front of the pulpit, grasping the Thompson Bible in one hand and gesturing with the other.

"God's mercy is available to you today, my friends. He sent His only Son to die on the cross for your sins. But you've got to accept His forgiveness and claim it for yourself. He's knocking on your heart's door. Open up and let Him come in."

The organist started the invitational hymn.

"Come to Jesus. Come now. Let Him save you, cleanse you, make you new. Drunkard, you come. Drug addict, you come. Adulterer, you come."

A stocky gray-haired man ran up the middle aisle crying. All over the church people were sobbing.

"Praise God! Here's a man coming to Jesus." Somebody go pray with him and help him to the light."

Another came. Another. Another. Until the altar was filled with people praying. Seven for salvation. About a dozen for restoration.

It was after one o'clock when we left the church. We had

another great service that night, and the outpouring of the Spirit continued through the week.

Carol and I were on our way.

During the next six years we crisscrossed the U.S. and Canada, north-south, east-west, holding revivals in small towns and big cities, singing and preaching in Assemblies of God youth camps and state conventions, leading city-wide crusades sponsored by groups of churches, seeing thousands come to Christ, witnessing many, many outpourings of God's Spirit.

Six hard, glory-filled years during which I received close-up, on-the-job-training for the ministry that no college or seminary could have ever provided.

I didn't intend it this way. I planned to start in Central Bible College in the fall of 1959. Four years at CBC or the equivalent in another acceptable study program was required for ordination. Until then I could only operate on a preacher's license which had to be renewed every year.

By summer I had so many revival invitations, I decided to postpone formal education for a year. The next year I was even busier.

I met the rest of the ordination requirements with correspondence courses from CBC, Crusader's Bible Institute, and the Moody Bible Institute. Not to mention the thousands of hours I spent reading commentaries and biographies of great preachers from Augustine to Billy Graham. It would be years before I received a formal degree, but I finally did, in 1975.

As a kid I had never really applied myself in school and it took me a while to learn how to study, but during those years there developed deep in my soul a passion for learning that will last the rest of my life. I'll never live long enough to learn all that I'd like to.

My first mentors were the host pastors where I held revivals. At night after service we usually had coffee and dessert at the parsonage. "What's one of your favorite sermons?" I frequently asked. The pastor would feel flattered and talk for hours about his messages. Later in our bedroom I'd write down the outlines. I picked up two or three good ideas in every revival that way.

Another valuable habit was looking through the pastor's library and asking which books were most helpful to him. I borrowed these books during the revival and if they seemed worthwhile I bought copies when we got a little extra money.

Back in Nashville between revivals I spent a good deal of time at the Carters'. Mother and Maybelle were best friends. My pal and teacher was E. J., Maybelle's husband.

E. J. didn't sing with the family, but worked on the railroad as a conductor. Our common interest was books and Bible knowledge. He had a library of several thousand volumes.

Typically, I found him sprawled on the floor of his study, five or six books on the subject he was researching spread out around him. We talked for hours at a time. On almost any question he could give me several Bible verses with background from history, psychology, and archaeology.

E. J. was one of the finest persons I ever knew. But I felt he needed a greater experience with Christ.

Sometimes I witnessed to him for an hour. On other occasions I didn't bring the matter up. It took a long time, but he finally came through to that deeper relationship with Jesus, became a regular attender at my home church and taught a class as long as his health permitted.

My education from correspondence, talking to preachers, reading, and E. J. Carter was strung out over a number of years. At the beginning of my ministry my Bible knowledge was very superficial and criticisms of shallowness were probably justified. Others were not.

For example some around Nashville said I went to preaching because I couldn't make it in show business. Ironically, I was also criticized for using show business techniques.

My show experience did help. I knew how to dress, sit, stand, and communicate with an audience. I had developed an instinct for rapport and timing. I could "take" an audience's pulse and sense when it was time to stop preaching—even if I was only halfway through my sermon outline—and give the altar call. But I never resorted to gimmicks which performers sometimes resort to on the stage. Why should I when the Holy Spirit does it all?

A complaint raised against both Carol and me was that we were riding on our parents' fame. We didn't intentionally do this, but during our first year some pastors played this connection up big to draw crowds. They ran advertisements such as: HEAR HANK SNOW'S SON PREACH AND WILMA LEE AND STONY COOPER'S DAUGHTER SING. Our names were in small print under our pictures. This was the type of thing that I had come to deeply resent before I was saved, when I had been trying to break away from dad. But as a young preacher it didn't bother me. It didn't bother Carol in regard to her folks either. And neither her parents nor mine ever objected.

After 1960 we were advertised in large print and our folks in small print. For this I mainly credit our good friend C. M. Ward, the beloved radio evangelist for the Assemblies' international broadcast "Revival Time." Dr. Ward wrote and published a mini-biography of us called "From Rock-and-Roll to a Passion for Souls." Forty-two thousand copies were mailed out to listeners on request and additional thousands sent to churches, schools, and camps. The booklet gave us a kind of official stamp of approval and created an aura of interest around us as former show business personalities.

With all this, I knew that it was not by might, nor by power, but by His Spirit that God's work was to be accomplished. Every afternoon in a revival I prayed from two to five-thirty, on my knees or walking around the empty auditorium talking to

God. Later in the evening I often prayed a couple of hours more. Carol would join me or play the organ.

There was plenty to pray for: strength to withstand temptations to preach for money and fame; requests of individuals who had come asking for prayer after services the night before; anointing upon the singing and preaching.

Pentecostals are not much for a formal order of service. They like to hang loose and let the Spirit lead. That bothered me. The same inspired apostle who said, "God hath chosen the foolish things of the world to confound the wise," also wrote, "Let all things be done decently and in order" (I Corinthians 1:27; 14:40). Pentecostals quote the first verse about as much, I suppose, as Presbyterians quote the second.

I believed in starting on time—something ingrained in me by dad. Sometimes it took a few reminders, but after a couple of nights the people learned that I wanted the warm-up congregational singing to begin precisely at seven-thirty. All the preliminaries—music, offering, and announcements—were to be completed by 8:00 when Carol and I came on the platform. We would sing a couple of numbers, and I would be into my sermon by 8:15.

I followed a typed or written sermon outline. Yes, I had heard the Scripture, "For I will give you a mouth and wisdom" (Luke 21:15). This promise was given to Christians brought into pagan courts and accused falsely. But I didn't let my sermon outline become a strait jacket around the Holy Spirit.

With all the sermon ideas picked up from pastors, I preached mostly on only sixteen standard subjects: prayer, soul winning, the Holy Spirit, salvation, judgment, and other great themes of Scripture. I preferred biblical illustrations to sticky sentimental tales that appeal only to the emotions.

However, I did have two specials, my testimony and a sermon on rock-and-roll music.

The rock-and-roll message was hatched in Plant City,

Florida, in October, 1961. The pastor heard me talking about old times and said, "You can help our young people. They're going crazy over this devilish stuff."

I ran down all the references in the Bible on music and found it mentioned both positively and negatively. First Samuel 16:23 says that David "took a harp and played with his hand; so Saul was refreshed, and was well, and the evil spirit departed from him." Second Samuel 6:5 states, "And David and all the house of Israel played before the Lord on all manner of instruments made of fir wood, even on harps, and on psalteries, and on timbrels, and on cornets, and on cymbals." Music was used to refresh the soul and to praise God.

But in Amos 6:4-6 the prophet heaped woe on those who "lie on beds of ivory . . . that chant to the sound of the viol . . . that drink wine in bowls." And I read in Daniel about Nebuchadnezzar commanding Shadrach, Meshach, and Abednego to bow down and worship the golden image when they heard the sound of his orchestra. This music, I felt, was demonic and designed to draw listeners into immorality. Only because they had the Spirit of God were the three Hebrews able to resist.

I announced on Monday night that I would be preaching on rock-and-roll the following Friday night. The church was jammed by seven o'clock. By seven-thirty there appeared to be more outside than inside the building.

I showed from the Bible how music could be used to glorify God or degrade man. Then I recalled what I had seen in rock-and-roll shows. Never did I indict any of the show business personalities in the rock-and-roll world. I stuck strictly to the music and its effects.

"Rock-and-roll primarily appeals to the sensual nature," I said. "It produces sexual hysteria in crowds and leads young people to surrender to the passions of the lower nature. It takes control of the mind and opens the door to drugs and illicit sex.

Don't try to tell me it doesn't. I know. I've been there."

"I warn you parents that rock-and-roll is creating a youth cult and driving a wedge between you and your children."

Turning back to the kids, I told them, "Only the Holy Spirit can deliver you from this demonic music. If you want to be set free tonight to serve God with a pure mind, come and let me pray for you. Then get rid of your records and sheet music."

"Let's have a burning and let the world know how we feel," a boy proposed. The suggestion swept through the church until the pastor with my concurrence announced a bonfire on the church grounds the next evening. Before an even larger crowd the kids burned hundreds of records, posters, and books, and then joined hands and sang praises to God for deliverance.

Nothing like this had ever happened in Florida, or perhaps anywhere else. The story was carried on the front pages of several area newspapers and picked up by the big wire services.

That night the Lord dealt with me. "You don't need this kind of publicity," He said.

I never sanctioned another public burning. But I felt freedom to continue preaching the special sermon.

The following February I was in a revival in Savannah, Georgia, with Glen Miller, the man who had been God's special messenger when I was trying to decide between show business and the ministry. A Savannah newspaper carried the announcement that I would preach Friday night on rock-and-roll.

Elvis Presley had just gotten out of the army and there was lots of speculation on whether he could pick up his career where he had left off. Someone at CBS-TV saw the Savannah story on my sermon, tied me to Elvis, and the result was the local CBS outlet sent a camera crew to film my sermon. Four minutes of it ran on the next national news.

Movie Screen magazine came out with an article titled,

"Does Elvis Know His Friends Are Still Praying for Him?" It gave the impression I had blasted him in the sermon, which wasn't true. I tried to reach Elvis through mutual friends to explain that I had meant nothing personal, but I never got through, and I have had no contact with him since.

The TV film clip is still circulating. I gave permission for it to be used in a nostalgic movie which played in Nashville a couple of years ago.

I preached the rock-and-roll sermon in most every revival after that. In one meeting a young preacher named Bob Larson pumped me for several hours afterwards. Even though he had only picked a guitar in a night club he developed a sermon on the subject and later wrote a book that sold well.

Audience response to the rock-and-roll message was favorable with only a few exceptions. One was a deacon who after hearing me announce the subject, dragged me before the other deacons. "You are not to preach that sermon here," he commanded, "or to talk about sexual matters from this pulpit."

To keep the peace, I agreed to substitute another message. That was a mistake. He was running the church, and I should have forced him into a showdown.

Before he left two years later he ruined that church. His daughter, who was heavy into rock-and-roll, got into big trouble.

In some churches I found the pastor on the hot seat because he had dared preach against sin. A pastor on the Gulf Coast confided he was risking his life by staying on. "Two of my deacons beat me up last week," he said. "And yesterday we came home from a trip and found ground glass in our sugar bowl."

The meeting in his church was one of the hardest I ever preached. There were only eighteen converted. But out of that eighteen came three Sunday school teachers, two God-fearing deacons, one Sunday school superintendent, two preachers, and a missionary. God knew what He was doing.

In some meetings sponsored by groups of churches the conversions ran into the hundreds. Two hundred came to the Lord during a tent crusade on the North Commons in my hometown of Halifax. My kinfolks came out of curiosity, but none were among those saved.

I never billed myself as a healer. I believed in divine healing, but I had serious reservations about many of the "divine healers."

While I didn't have separate healing services, I always had a prayer line for people with special problems—unemployment, marital difficulties, sickness, drinking, whatever was troubling them. I stood on the platform and prayed briefly for each person, then asked the pastor or a layman to take them aside for extended prayer and counsel. I didn't want people to get a fixation on me as a guru with a special connection to the Almighty.

I laid hands on thousands of people and caught a disease only once. This was in Sidonia, Tennessee. Within a week my body was covered with a burning, itching rash.

By this time I was in a revival in West Nashville. I swathed my body with sulfa ointment and put on my wool suit—the only winter suit I owned at the time. The heat blowers were just behind the pulpit. When I stepped up to preach, the scent hit the congregation like a truckload of rotten eggs. The prayer line was short every night.

My primary aim was always to get people saved. But beyond the thousands of conversions, I witnessed some other miracles that couldn't be questioned. Marriages restored. Parents and children reunited. Jobs provided. Sick persons healed.

I saw a woman in Enterprise, Alabama, whose heart was so bad her doctors had given her only six to eight months to live. Friends carried her into the church where the pastor and I and several other members laid hands on her and asked God for healing. When I met her three years later she was teaching a Sunday school class in apparent good health.

But I also saw devout Christians pray and pray and pray and still go away sick. Many are dead now. It was God's will to take them on to heaven.

I never pretended to understand the theology of healing. I knew that it was in God's hands.

I always felt the biggest miracle was salvation. I saw drunks turn sober, unfaithful husbands become faithful and start loving their wives, kids get delivered from drugs, and many other types of transformations—all through the new birth and the power of the Spirit. I preached the promise: "If any man be in Christ, he is a new creature" (II Corinthians 5:17). Praise God, I saw it happen again and again.

Many came to hear me because of my background in show business and stayed to get saved. A few came because they had known me in the old days.

One old friend came with her son to a meeting in Jacksonville, Florida. I didn't know she was there until I saw her coming to the altar with her son.

"Suzy! Suzy Caldwell!" I yelled loud enough to be heard across the building and gave her a big hug.

"We're coming to get saved, Jimmy," she sobbed.

"Just ask Jesus to forgive your sins and come into your hearts," I encouraged. "He died on the cross for your sins and mine. He'll save you just as He saved me. He will, I know He will."

Her tears rained down on the carpet, "Lord, forgive me. Lord take me. I'm not fit, but take me. Lord, Lord, Lord. . . ."

Remembering the hours we had spent together back in the beer joint in Nashville, I was too choked to speak.

She looked up at me, her face shining. "Oh, Jimmy, I believe. I believe. I know He died for me. And my son, too."

"Praise God! Praise God!" was all I could say.

I had to go over and pray with someone else. After the service we got together briefly.

"How's Harry?" I asked.

A shadow crossed her face. "I really don't know. We divorced after you left us. I just couldn't take his drinking anymore. If we had been saved, it might have been different."

"We'll have to pray for him," I said.

"Yes," she murmured, "we certainly will."

The pastor was closing up the church. "You were always a good friend, Suzy," I told her. "You weren't saved, but you listened to me. You seemed to care."

"I guess I felt sorry for you. Maybe it was my motherly instinct. I worried about you lots. And I always wondered what happened to you. Then I heard you were to preach a revival in this church. I had to come."

"Did you ever think I'd become a preacher?"

"No, Jimmy, never. Not in my wildest imagination."

9
The "Flip" Side of Evangelism

You rarely read a multi-sided presentation of the life of an evangelist, particularly the life of a Pentecostal one. It's either a sanitized religious version that has everybody coming up holy and spouting King James, or a "Gantry version" that depicts the preacher as a phony out to fleece the poor innocent sheep who don't know any better.

I'm not pretending to be totally objective. No one can be. But I am trying to be fair and honest in relating my personal experiences in evangelism and reactions to situations some of the brethren don't like to talk about.

When I was converted and entered the ministry I swung from one extreme to another. From a whiskey-guzzling, pill-popping, profligate playboy, I flipped to a no-drinking, no-cussing, no-smoking, no-movies, no-dancing, no-TV, no-mixed swimming, no-card-playing square.

I knew next to nothing about Pentecostalism or any other evangelical group for that matter. It was some time before I understood the reasons for the origin of this first renewal movement in twentieth century Protestantism. Pentecostalism resulted from a revivalistic reaction to coldness and sterility in the established churches. Hungry people began to seek God and the result was a split in the first decade of the century from main line denominations over the doctrine of the Holy Spirit. Unfortunately this led to excesses in ascetic living, other-worldliness, and legalism which characterized the Assemblies of God in the 1960's.

I entered the Assemblies as a babe in Christ. I thought this was the only way to go for dedicated Christians, especially preachers. And I wanted to be dedicated.

In retrospect I have no keen regrets. The discipline was good for me. I think if I had gotten into a good-Lord, good-Devil type of church where anything goes, I might have slid back into my old ways.

I wasn't in the Assemblies long, however, before I recognized that much of what they taught was excessive. In East Texas, for example, I went to preach at a youth camp. They were filling in the swimming pool with concrete. I was puzzled. They explained that the camp had been purchased from another denomination that believed in mixed bathing. They didn't.

It seemed that some of the prohibitions invited hypocrisy. I knew one old deacon who ranted and raved against TV and refused to have one in his house. But when his favorite programs came on he simply slipped down the street and watched at a neighbor's.

I was automatically suspect because I had been in show business. Some preachers checked on my worldliness quotient with the district superintendent in Nashville. "Does he watch TV?" "Does he go to the movies?" The superintendent wasn't the type to split hairs and he couldn't always give the answers they wanted.

I was warned in advance about a pastor who suspected we carried a TV with us. I decided to give him a hard time.

When we arrived he was anxious to help us unload our trailer. "No, thanks, brother," I said. "We're going to rest awhile before taking the stuff in."

We went on into the little apartment which the church had reserved for us and lay down.

He kept coming back every few minutes, wondering if we were ready. After he left the third time we ran to the trailer and moved the gear in fast. We had just closed the door when we heard a noise outside. I slipped up and opened the door a crack. "Oh, Brother Snow," he giggled. "I just came to see if you need anything."

"Not a thing, brother," I said. "We're well taken care of." Carol was lying on the bed, about to crack up.

About fifteen minutes later we heard him creeping back. I sneaked to the door and caught him again. This happened a half-dozen times that week. He never did find out if we were guilty. I almost wished we had had a little portable with us.

Apparently he wasn't as concerned about his marital relations. In the church he and his wife were lovey dovey. In the parsonage they fought like alley cats. One night she got so angry at him that she fell on the living room floor and kicked her feet in frustration while Carol and I looked on.

Women gave me a lot of flack about Carol. One old sister in Mississippi who wore long sleeves in the hottest weather and her hair in a bun slipped up to me and whispered, "Brother Snow, your little wife is so sweet. I just love to hear her sing. But I'm afraid she'll give our young girls the wrong idea."

"What's that, sister?" I asked.

"Well, she wears her hair so short. Couldn't you speak to her about letting it grow. You know what Paul said to the women at Corinth. How that it was a shame for women to cut their hair."

"Sister, why don't you speak to her yourself?"

"Oh, Brother Snow, I couldn't be that direct. Besides, aren't you the head of your house?"

"Yes, sister, but if she offends you, I think you should tell her. She'll listen."

"No, no, she doesn't offend me. I was just worried about the young girls."

"Are any of them your daughters?"

"No. Mine are all grown up and gone."

"Then their mothers should see that they look decent. Excuse me, sister, I've got to work on my sermon. It was nice talking to you."

Others complained that Carol's dresses were too tight or too short or that she wore too much makeup. I felt Carol dressed very modestly and tastefully and I knew she never wore makeup. I think they were just jealous of her talent and good looks.

Some of the preachers' wives treated Carol like a Cinderella stepchild. They insisted that she help them mop floors and wash dishes—"to keep you humble, child," one said. Carol did as they asked.

The eating and sleeping arrangements were quite a switch from show tours where we had stayed in good hotels.

We never knew where we would be eating or what. During one two-week revival, we took every meal in a different home and had fried chicken twice a day except for two meals. I thought I'd grow feathers before we left that place.

The most unforgettable eating experience happened in Houston, Texas, where the hostess took us immediately into the kitchen. "We'uns is jist poor folks. Don't have any living room furniture," she said.

The pastor and his wife and Carol and I sat down with her husband and made small talk. "Dinner is acomin' along," the woman assured. "We'uns don't have much. We hope ye like it."

She pulled from the oven a fat duck her husband had shot that morning. It was black with hair sticking out all over and stunk so bad I wanted to throw up before I took a bite. I glanced at the pastor and saw his face yellowing.

She jerked off a leg and laid it on my plate alongside a helping of lumpy, watery potatoes. "Would you like a glass of milk to go with that, Brother Snow?" Praise the Lord, I said, "No thank you, sister, I'll have some water." When she dipped the pastor some milk from a wash basin, I saw the scum fall off the glass.

He was about to gag. "Uh, it's a little warm. Would you open the door and give us some air, Brother Snow?" he asked.

I opened it gladly.

The woman sat down grinning. "I guess we're all ready to dig in." She nodded at her husband and he said to me, "Brother Snow, will you do us the honor by asking the blessin'?"

I prayed. Oh, how I prayed.

I don't mean to leave the impression that all the hospitality was this bad. Most places the home cooking was delicious. In many homes we realized that the family had really sacrificed to feed us.

During the first two or three years Carol and I took everything in stride, the good along with the bad, sometimes laughing, sometimes groaning when we were alone. We were serving the Lord, battling the devil, winning souls. We could survive a little discomfort along the way. But after a while I began to insist that the matter of accommodations be settled before I would accept an invitation to preach.

It was the same with offerings. For the first couple of years, I told pastors, "Whatever the Lord provides will be all right with us."

I left it up to the preachers to take the offering. I was sensitive to criticism and also wanted to concentrate on the sermon.

Most pastors would say, "Now we know Brother and Sister Snow aren't here for the money, but if the Lord puts something on your heart to give, they'll appreciate it." That kind of appeal seldom filled the basket.

Most of the people we preached to were not well off financially. A hundred dollars a week was a big salary to a lot of folks. They didn't consider that we might have to travel five hundred miles to the next meeting, and that without a good offering we would have to drive all night because we couldn't afford a motel. Maybe it was pride, but I just couldn't bring myself to talk about money for quite a while.

What precipitated a change in policy was a growing awareness that some money given for our ministry was not coming to us.

I was becoming vaguely suspicious about this when, one day, we started a two-week meeting in a congregation of about five hundred members. We had a good revival, over forty were saved, and there were that many more restorations of faith. During the two weeks one man mentioned that he had put fifty dollars in the basket for us and a woman said she and her husband had given a hundred dollars. Together with other gifts we heard about, we were counting on at least four hundred dollars—money we needed to catch up the slack from a couple of small churches.

Imagine our surprise when the pastor handed us a check for only $134. I was so hurt, I didn't know what to say.

The next month we were at a camp meeting where I shared the pulpit with another evangelist. I told him my sad story and asked what he knew about that kind of thing. He said, "Man, don't you know? The preacher or treasurer gave you what they thought you should have, not what the people gave. The treasurer may have figured the church needed to catch up on bills. Or the pastor felt he should share in the revival proceeds."

"I wouldn't object to that if they told the people. But they asked the people to give for our ministry. Why, that's stealing," I snorted.

"They don't see it that way. But it is taking funds under false pretenses. Used to happen to me all the time."

"How did you handle the problem?" I asked.

"I started specifying a minimum amount when a pastor would call me for a revival. I would tell him if the church can't pay that much, then they don't want me. And then I'd insist that whatever is received for my ministry comes to me. If they need money for something else, they should tell the people. The ones with integrity don't mind. And it keeps the rest from yielding to temptation."

After that I started asking pastors who called about meetings, "What is your minimum pay?" If it wasn't enough I would explain, "I'm not putting a price on my ministry, but I have certain financial obligations I must meet to maintain my integrity." Often if the church could not afford to pay more, and other offerings had been good, we'd go anyway.

It was disillusioning to learn of evangelists who were less than paragons of virtue and honesty, although this shock was cushioned by the Nashville preacher who had disappointed me at the start of my ministry. These fellows invariably took their own offering, making appeals that would melt the Rock of Gibraltar. Some took away thousands of dollars from meetings sponsored by only six to eight small churches, leaving the pastors to catch the criticism.

I met some of these charlatans. Others I heard about from pastors whose sheep had been shorn.

One traveling evangelist told me that divine unction wasn't necessary for him. "I can anoint myself and go on," he declared.

I knew I could never pull that off even if I had wanted to. I just didn't have the natural ability to communicate that some have. My reliance had to be completely on the power of the Spirit. I could never bluff it.

Another evangelist suggested I was a fool not to get on the

gravy train. "With your knowledge of show business, you can pull in a hundred thousand a year. Maybe more," he said.

"Look," I replied bluntly, "if I were going to go that route, I'd go back to show business."

The tricks I heard about were nauseating.

A West Coast preacher displayed pickled frogs and animal embryos in jars of formaldehyde and claimed they were demons he had cast out of people. This crook, who preached that alcohol was a ruination, died in a drunken stupor.

Another had his microphone wiring rigged so he could give "charges" to persons as they came through the healing line. Holding the mike with one hand, he would say piously, "I feel the healing power of God flowing through my body," and touch the seeker's forehead. Wham! The person would shout, "Praise the Lord!"

I saw a lot of programmed emotionalism. One preacher had a "Holy Ghost rubdown" to help people get filled with the Spirit. Another had a "falling-out-in-the-Spirit" night.

Marjo is a special case. He was the young man who turned from preaching to acting a few years ago, claiming he had been trained by his parents since childhood to put on an act. Marjo has since written a book and become something of a celebrity. He tells people who don't believe in God or the Bible what they want to hear. He eases their guilty consciences.

I don't say Marjo isn't honest in the context of his own experience. I agree that there are others still on the circuit who are just as fake as he was. I commend him for having the courage to quit pretending and admit that his preaching and healing were all a farce.

A couple of years ago I met Marjo. He was subbing for Dick Cavett and came by to interview dad. I happened to be at the house. The time was too brief to get to know him. And even if he had been there longer, I wouldn't have collared him.

I did have the opportunity of getting to know his father

recently when I preached for him out in California. I found him to be a delightful man. Just the opposite of the impression Marjo gives of him.

I'd love to sit down with Marjo sometime and share experiences. I'd like to ask him if he's happier now, if he's found peace, if he has discovered the meaning for life everyone seeks.

And if he's really interested, I'd like to show him how to find the real truth that will set him free. The existence of false religion doesn't invalidate the true. A counterfeit, for example, only points to and relies upon the existence of the real thing.

Show business was a way of life for my family. At age eleven I'm relaxing between shows with dad and mother.

As an entertainer and a preacher, I've known most of the living legends in country music. "Big Slim" was one of the most unique. Part of his act was cracking a whip across the stage to cut a cigarette in half–in his wife's mouth.

I was sent to three schools during the ninth grade, my last year in public school. The school authorities never knew what to do about me.

A guide at Independence Hall shows dad and me the famous Liberty Bell. We still love our native Canada, but we're proud today to be naturalized citizens of the United States.

At twenty-one I had everything the world says should make you happy. Friends in show biz like Elvis Presley, money, a famous name, and a beautiful girl who said she would marry me. And yet I had nothing. Booze and pills had me totally enslaved. . . . Even dad had given up on me.

"Of course, I know how to ride a motorcycle," I told dad. It was a lie. Only the mercy of God kept me alive that winter.

A drunken driver in a stolen car traveling at 105 miles per hour hit me head-on. This is what was left of my '54 Olds. It was a miracle I survived.

After my accident was announced at the Opry, mail began to pour in. We stopped counting at ten thousand cards and letters.

Preaching up a storm on the "sawdust trail." CBS filmed my sermon denouncing rock and roll, and broadcast excerpts of it on their network evening news program.

Elvis with my girl Carol Cooper and me backstage at the Opry. He invited me to spend a couple of weeks with him in Memphis and I accepted.

"Gospel Country" was the second most popular Sunday morning TV show in the Nashville area. Trio members: me, Carol and Larry King.

Connie Smith on the "Grand Ole Gospel Time." Jimmie Riddle is to her right, in back. Elaine Tubb, an old friend from my teen-age days at the Opry, stands on the choir riser in back of Jimmie.

Hawkshaw Hawkins, along with two other Opry entertainers, was killed in a plane crash. Hawkshaw and I were good friends. Only a few days before his death he had promised me that he would be in church the next Sunday.

Hank Snow, my dad, appearing on "Grand Ole Gospel Time."

Dennis Weaver, the singer and actor who played the unforgettable Chester on "Gunsmoke" for many years, sings for the Lord on "Grand Ole Gospel Time."

I'll never forget the day John Cash came to the altar at Evangel Temple. I had preached on Acts 16:31, emphasizing that a father should lead his family in faith. John walked forward, followed by his wife, June, and their children. In this picture his father and old pastor stand in background.

I was invited to give the prayer before the House of Representatives on the very day, as it turned out, that President Nixon announced his resignation. Left to right: Congressman Richard Fulton from Nashville, the House chaplain, myself, my wife Dottie and Carl Albert, the Speaker of the House.

My wife Dottie is also from a country music family. Old-timers will remember her parents, Dot and Smokey Swan (shown at center microphone), who performed on the Opry for many years. To their left is "Bashful Brother" Oswald and, beyond him on their extreme left, is the one and only Roy Acuff.

Dottie, loving wife and loyal helpmate. She came into my life when I needed her most.

10
Coming Home

The Assemblies accepted Carol and me because we had made a clean break with show business. The consensus in the denomination was that you couldn't live for God and be a worldly entertainer.

I had some fierce arguments with preachers about that.

"The Bible says, 'come out from among them and be ye separate,' " one pastor declared. "Anyone who means business with God will get off the stage."

"That makes about as much sense as saying a farmer should quit farming or a plumber should quit plumbing," I countered.

"That's not a good comparison, Brother Snow. Stage music is a worldly profession."

"Don't you ever listen to the Grand Ole Opry or some other country music program on the radio?"

I had him, but he wouldn't admit it. "Well, maybe once in a while, when I'm driving and can't find a gospel program. But that's different."

"Didn't the singing help you relax and pass the time?"

"I guess it did. But I still think consecrated Christians will get off the stage."

"Brother," I said, trying to remain patient, "I'll admit some entertainers are wicked. Just as some plumbers are."

"Not as many, Brother Snow. Not as many."

"The reason you say that is when an entertainer gets messed up with a woman everybody hears about it. When a plumber steps out of line, all he loses is a little business. His kinfolks may not even find out."

There was a gleam in the preacher's eye. "Then why don't you go back to show business?"

"Because God called me into full-time ministry. That's His will for me. I can't speak for anybody else."

I never felt show business in itself was evil. There was decent entertainment and indecent entertainment, but I had to concede that not many entertainers were really living for God. At least not so far as I could tell. About as far as most went was to sing an occasional sacred song. This concerned me and I prayed often for those I had been associated with in show business.

I was home between revivals when the phone jangled early one morning.

"Praise the Lord!" a deep growl shouted in my ear. I'd heard that growl before, but. . . .

"Who is this?"

"Praise the Lord!"

"Who in the world is this?"

"Don't you know your old pal, son? It's Tex Tyler."

T. Texas Tyler. My old roommate on a number of show tours. A real old-timer who had sung in many western movies. In a class with Bob Wills, Eddy Arnold, and Jimmie Davis, Tex had written a number-one hit song in the forties called "A Deck of Cards" which took him to Carnegie Hall.

I was coming awake, remembering the last time I'd been

with Tex. San Antonio. We had just done an afternoon matinee. I hadn't gone back to the room before the evening show. Tex had and ran into a clutch of lawmen. They got him for smuggling drugs across the Mexican border. Stuck him in a padded cell. Tex didn't make the show that night, and I hadn't seen him since.

"Tex, what happened to you?"

"I'm saved, son. I got saved in my cell. The Lord got me out of jail and I'm preaching just like you. Praise the Lord!"

Tex lived only about three years more, but they were spent for God and I look forward to seeing him in heaven.

On the rare Saturday nights when we weren't away in a revival, Carol and I went down to the Opry to visit backstage. The oldtimers treated us like family.

The Opry was growing and it seemed every time we went we were introduced to a newcomer. It wasn't my nature to buttonhole a person and ask, "Are you saved?" I waited for an opportunity to sit down in private and share the gospel.

One who really listened was Patsy Cline. Patsy's recordings of "Walking after Midnight" and "I Fall to Pieces" were climbing the charts and the fan magazines were calling her the "queen of country music." Yet Patsy confessed to me that the fame hadn't satisfied and her life was unfulfilled.

I had to leave for a revival and encouraged her to attend the Assembly of God in Madison. She was saved there early in 1963.

Another I talked to around this time was Cowboy Copas, who was making hay with "Filipino Baby" and "Hillbilly Heaven." I knew Cowboy and his family well. His son, Gary, and I had run around together before I was saved. I was also good friends with Randy Hughes, Cowboy's pilot son-in-law. Cowboy was a decent, honest man, better than some church people I had known, but he was noncommittal about spiritual matters.

I occasionally stopped off to see Hawkshaw and Jean Hawkins at their house near Dickerson Road. Jean came to hear me preach when I was holding revivals in Nashville and Hawkshaw was always going to come. He was an old friend from West Virginia days and was now doing well on the Opry.

The last time I saw Hawkshaw was in February, 1963. We sat in his den and talked about priorities. The black jacket with the hawk emblem on the back which he wore on stage was draped over a chair. He was in a reflective mood.

"Jimmie, I've never told anybody in Nashville this before, but when I was a boy back in West Virginia God touched my heart to be an evangelist. I loved the music business so much that I ran out of the church and never went back."

"How's it been with you since?" I asked.

"I've gone further in my career than I ever dreamed. But I've always known something was missing."

"What's missing is the Lord, Hawkshaw. He'll reveal His will to you after you turn your life over to Him."

His face spread in a resolute smile. "I know that, Jimmy, and I've made up my mind. Cowboy and Patsy and I are going on a long tour. Our last show will be a benefit for the family of Cactus Jack in Kansas City. He's an old deejay buddy who was killed in an automobile accident. When I get home, I promise you, I'm starting back to church the next Sunday."

Then he stood up and circled the date on a wall calendar, March 9, 1963.

I continued to pray for Hawkshaw and other friends. On March 6, I heard the terrible news that shook the Opry. Hawkshaw, Cowboy, Patsy, and Randy Hughes, their pilot, had run into bad weather between Dyersburg and Nashville the evening before. Early the next morning a fire tower watchman spotted the Piper Comanche and gave directions to a search crew. They knew it was them when they saw Hawkshaw's black jacket sticking out of the wreckage.

About a year later another good Opry friend, Jim Reeves, also died in a plane crash. Jim Reeves had lived right behind dad and mother in Madison and we had worked a lot of shows together.

He wasn't the last. Altogether, eight members of the Opry died in four accidents in 1963 and 1964.

These tragedies cemented in my mind the conviction that God wanted me to come back to Nashville and start a church that would reach into the country music community.

Preacher friends warned that one's hometown was the hardest place of all to pioneer a ministry. One said point blank, "I don't think you can cut the mustard."

There was another consideration. Carol and I now had a daughter, born September 19, 1962, while I was holding a revival in St. Louis. Three weeks after Vanessa's birth, mother and daughter were back on the evangelism circuit. Our beautiful brown-haired, blue-eyed doll was never any trouble. We set her bassinet on the platform and went on with the services while she slept.

But we knew Vanessa would have to start school in a few years. I would have to settle down or be away from my family for weeks at a time.

This burden was still weighing heavily on me the next spring when the district council met at the First Assembly in Madison for my ordination. Those who were to be ordained sat in the front row of the crowded building while J. Robert Ashcroft, the President of Evangel College at that time, brought a message from the first Psalm. The service was one of the real highlights of my life. Yet even while hands were being laid upon me I felt this constraining desire to reach the people of Nashville.

I put out a "fleece." "Lord, if you want me to start a church in Nashville, have some churches ask me to be their pastor. Then I'll know it's time to leave evangelism."

Not one church had ever asked me, and I had preached

several revivals in churches where the pastors had recently left.

A year passed and still no invitations to pastor. In June, 1965, Carol and I finished a two-week meeting in a large Oklahoma City church and started driving toward the Arkansas border. The future looked very promising. We were getting into the biggest churches of the denomination and I had recently preached my fourteenth state convention sermon. I was beginning to think the Lord wanted us to stay in evangelism.

As we started out of town, I had a nagging feeling that we had closed the revival too soon. I mentioned this to Carol and she said, "Well, let's go back." I turned around at the next corner and went back and called the pastor.

"I feel the same way," he responded. "In fact, I've been trying to locate you."

We started calling key church leaders, asking them to spread the word. That week turned out to be the best of the three. But what really struck me was that I received calls to pastor from several churches in different parts of the country. None in six years and now several in one week.

We went straight home and I called the pastors of the churches where we were scheduled for revivals the rest of the summer. They all agreed to put their meetings ahead so I would have the summer free.

After a few days' rest I went to see the Assemblies' superintendent. He was encouraging, but pointed out a couple of denominational rules. A new work had to be at least three miles from an existing Assembly of God and it had to have twenty-one members to receive a charter. He suggested I ask Assembly pastors around Nashville for advice on possible locations.

I knew the preachers well and had held revivals for most of them. The one on the east side said, "Brother Snow, you ought to look on the west side." The one on the south side felt the north side of town would be best. Etc. Etc. I knew they were worried about losing sheep and wanted me as far away as possible.

Carol and I drove around for days. The area around Dickerson Road and Old Hickory Boulevard seemed the least churched. It was a little far from the center of town but growing fast. And quite a few music people lived close by. It was pretty close to our home church in Madison but Brother Alford told us to go ahead and look for property.

We found a four-acre site for $40,000 on Dickerson between two of my old hangouts, Caldwell's Tavern and the Starlight Club. From $1,500 saved from our six years in evangelism, I put up $600 for a 90-day option. Then I used the balance of the savings plus a loan on insurance policies to rent a tent, five hundred chairs, an organ, and a public address system. Members from the church in Madison and other Nashville congregations came and built a platform.

My plan was to preach for a month, then invite new converts living in the area to be the nucleus for the new church. I felt confident there would be at least a hundred to start the church with.

We launched a publicity campaign. Carol and I sang and talked up the church on TV and radio talk shows. The newspapers did feature stories. Opry friends promised to make personal appearances.

The tent was packed and people were converted almost every night. My optimism rose. Surely we'd have a hundred, maybe a hundred and fifty to start the new church.

I closed the meeting the last Saturday night in September after announcing that the first services for the new church would be held the next morning. "We don't want anybody to come who already has a church home," I reminded.

Eight people came. Carol and I made ten. Eleven short of the charter requirements.

I was crestfallen and ready to go back into evangelism. Or

else take one of the out-of-town churches that had invited me to be their pastor.

I went and talked to my pastor. "You've got forty-five days on your option. Why not try it a few more Sundays," he counseled.

The next Sunday four or five new people came and by the end of the month twenty-three had pledged to become members of a new church.

We turned the tent and most of the chairs back to the rental company and kept the organ and about thirty-five chairs. Our accumulated offerings were enough to pay seventy-five dollars for a month's rent for one side of a small office building farther south on Dickerson. With an adjoining office which auctioneer Wayne Hawley let us use on Sunday, we had space for three Sunday school classes. I taught the teenagers and adults and Carol and Jay Jackson, Pastor Alford's brother-in-law, had two children's classes in the auctioneer's office. Then Carol played the organ for worship services and I preached.

We batted around several names and settled on Evangel Temple, the name of a church Carol and I had visited in Florida. I liked the ring of the name. It suggested a center of evangelism.

We now had a congregation and a name and enough offering to pay the rent with a few dollars left over. Not nearly enough to pay the pastor a salary. And not a fraction of the amount needed to purchase property and build a building. Even if we could get a loan.

The option had only a few days to run when I went over to discuss a small matter with dad. Carol and I were now living in our own house next door on the lot my folks had given us as a wedding present.

I had long been back in dad's good graces, and reinstated in his will and insurance policies. In fact, I learned that he had never really written me out of them, and had only told me he had in an attempt to shake me out of my delinquency. But he had never come to hear me preach.

We transacted our business quickly. I was leaving when he called me back.

"Are you serious about starting this church?"

I assured him we were and that we already had enough members for the charter.

"How much is the property?"

"I put six hundred on the option. That leaves $39,400."

"Then I'll lend the money and when the church is able, it can pay me back without interest over a four year span."

You could have knocked me over. I had no idea this was coming. I could only say, "Yes, sir, thank you very much." And, "Praise God!"

Dad wrote a check. We bought the property.

Dad was agreeable for the property to be collateral for a bond issue that would pay for a building. An Assemblies preacher from Memphis, who was also a builder, offered to arrange for the bonds and supervise the building with the church acting as general contractor. He said the church could get better bids from subs and buy materials cheaper than he could. He suggested a $75,000 issue with $5,000 set aside to pay the pastor a hundred-dollar weekly salary for the first year. "By then you'll have a building and enough offering to make the bond payments and pick up your salary," he predicted.

It sounded like a good deal, but it would be tough on my family. We had been accustomed to living on about two hundred dollars a week from revival income. This would mean a fifty per cent cut and we wouldn't have any savings to fall back on. We knew our parents would help us in a real bind, but neither of us wanted that. Still Carol went along as she always had with my decisions.

The preacher-builder was to provide blueprints. "What do you want?" he asked over coffee in a restaurant.

I had three things in mind. "Good acoustics with plenty of electrical outlets around the platform for a band. The floor sloping as in a theater so the congregation will be looking down at the preacher and choir. And make the sanctuary wide instead of long to create a better sense of closeness."

I sketched on a napkin an octagonal shaped building with the roof rising steeply to a pinnacle in the center. Offices and nursery behind the platform. Sunday school rooms in the basement underneath. With the lot sloping steeply downhill from Dickerson, the basement would be at ground level in the back.

He had the plans drawn and the church approved them.

Now to sell the bonds which came in denominations from $250 to $1,000. Most of my friends were entertainers. I made a list and began telephoning for appointments. "Got something I'd like to talk to you about. It'll just take a few minutes of your time. Where can I meet you?" I went to their offices, homes, backstage at the Opry, anywhere I could make a pitch.

I caught Johnny Cash backstage at the Municipal Auditorium where he and June were preparing to do a show. He popped a beer can as I entered and was high as a kite, but he listened respectfully as I explained what the bonds were for and that they would pay six per cent interest. "Sounds good to me, Jimmy," he said. "Put us down for $4,000."

I met Billy Walker for lunch at Shoney's restaurant in Madison. Billy had come to the Opry from the "Big D Jamboree" in Dallas where dad had once performed. We were old friends.

As we talked, Billy expressed an interest in more than just church bonds.

"I'm miserable the way I am," he told me.

I told him what the Lord had done for me. "If He could help me, He can sure help you," I said.

"Just tell me how."

I did and suggested that we pray right in the booth. "Just ask

Jesus to save you, Billy. The Bible promises in Romans that whosoever will call upon the Lord will be saved."

We joined hands across the table and prayed, ignoring the stares around us.

Billy looked up smiling. "It's all right, Jimmy. I'll see you in church Sunday."

He bought some bonds, too.

It took a long time to sell the entire issue. Carol's folks, who had long since accepted me as their son-in-law, made a purchase, as did about twenty other Opry members. The last denominations were finally purchased by a widow who used a portion of her inheritance.

Billy Walker, who later became famous for "Charlie's Shoes," was the first performer to join the church. Through contacts and friendships Carol and I had made through the years, we began reaching other performers and their families.

Lefty and Alice Frizzell came next. Alice was saved but Lefty never joined. He was a real old-timer around Nashville and had a lot of big hits.

Alice brought Dot Kilgore to church. Dot and her husband Merle, who wrote the song "Ring of Fire" that put Johnny Cash in lights, were having marital problems at the time. They subsequently divorced. Dot took her troubles to the Lord and became a faithful member of Evangel Temple.

The building was now under construction. We were eager to get in it. The rented office was much too small. As soon as we got a roof over the basement and a nursery above it, we moved in.

Everything was fine until one Sunday morning we walked in and found a lake. We had to get brooms and sweep the mess out before we could start Sunday school.

Every time it rained the basement flooded. The legs of our new chairs quickly rusted. Children dirtied their new shoes. Water would run under our feet.

Regrading the lot solved the water problem. But now the preacher-overseer seemed to be stalling, and sub-contractors and suppliers were calling about unpaid bills.

I finally got him on the phone. "Don't worry, I've got everything under control," he assured. "I'll be there next week and will pay the bills. We'll get that auditorium up."

He came and left again. The bills remained unpaid.

I did a little investigating, which I should have done in the beginning, and found he had three more jobs going.

The church demanded an accounting of the use of our bond funds. A few days later he called back to report his house had burned destroying all the building records of the four churches.

He couldn't explain how the money had been spent. We suspected he had been robbing Peter to pay Paul and had used some of our money on the other jobs. But we couldn't prove a thing. I mentally kicked myself for being so incredibly naive.

The bond money was gone, we owed $23,000 and the building wasn't finished. I explained our quandry to our creditors and begged for patience. God bless them, they waited, while we scrimped and saved.

We were really in a pickle. Our offerings couldn't go up until we could accommodate more people. We couldn't increase attendance until the auditorium was finished.

We could only pay and pray and work. Day and night, six days a week you could hear hammers and saws until, hallelujah, the auditorium was ready.

What a great day it was when my old friend, radio evangelist C. M. Ward, came and dedicated the building. By 1968 attendance was pushing two hundred. Six or eight were being saved every Sunday. We were making headway with the old debts and also paying dad back for the property loan. Dad, bless him, was putting as much into the church as he was receiving on the debt.

Evangel Temple had never been a typical Assembly of God. We were reaching folks from many religious backgrounds, mostly Baptist, Presbyterian, Methodist, and Pentecostal. I found it wasn't easy to pastor people with such diversity in doctrine and life style.

Some held strongly to the Calvinistic tenet of once saved, always saved, while those raised under Arminian theology believed salvation could be lost. Pentecostal traditionalists felt going to a movie was a terrible sin. The Baptists couldn't see any difference between going to a theater and watching TV. By this time most Pentecostals had come around to accept TV.

In the worship services the Pentecostals liked whooping and hollering and shouting which upset the Presbyterians. Sometimes I felt I was pastor of several congregations.

By preaching expository Bible sermons and pushing soul winning, I kept down the doctrinal hassles, but keeping everybody happy in worship was more of a problem. Actually the Pentecostal element was the biggest pain. If there wasn't dancing in the aisles and speaking in tongues on Sunday, they'd be complaining on Monday about how cold the service was. "This isn't the way we want it," they griped.

I raked them over the coals in a sermon. "What are we here for?" I asked rhetorically. "We're here to get folks saved and to help Christians grow, not to run a circus. If the Spirit makes you shout, go ahead and shout. If He leads you to speak in tongues, find an interpreter so we can all be blessed. But don't make a fleshly show and work up a lot of emotion just because you think you have to worship a certain way."

I lost some Pentecostals over that. They went to other churches where they could "enjoy" their religion more.

The church had just settled down again when the treasurer raised a ruckus about the pastor not going through proper channels to spend church money. I got a little huffy and said she was impugning my honesty. One word led to another. The treasurer resigned and took a half dozen members with her.

Again, chalk it up to ignorance and inexperience.

I was learning that it's a lot tougher to be a pastor than an evangelist. At Evangel Temple I couldn't leave my mistakes behind after two weeks. I had to live with them day after day.

11
Church of the Stars

The birth pains of Evangel Temple seemed behind us in 1968 when the church "took off" in attendance. This in a city that, besides being the world capital of country music, is headquarters for seven denominations, one of the largest Protestant publishing centers in the world, and, according to many preachers, a gospel-hardened graveyard of evangelism.

My vision expanded. I foresaw a church of five to seven thousand members with a radio and television ministry, a Christian school complex with grades from kindergarten through seminary, a corps of evangelists, and a star-studded cast of born-again country musicians who would speak for Christ from Nashville to Carnegie Hall.

I believed we were well on our way.

We had three evangelistic services, Sunday morning and night and Thursday night. Live, Spirit-filled services. Toe-tapping music. Roof-lifting singing. Testifying and praising God. Freedom to preach an hour or more. Altar-filled climaxes with hugging and shouting. And a Friday evening prayer meeting that often lasted all night.

You didn't have to dress to fit a mold. Long hair or short, makeup or plain, dresses or pants suits, Levis or business suits—everybody was welcome to come as they wished, so long as they were modest.

With Carol's and my background, it was natural that Evangel Temple take on a strong country music flavor. When the choir and band made a "joyful noise unto the Lord" the platform looked like a little Grand Ole Opry.

Nowhere in Nashville, except at the Opry, could you find such a variety of country musicians. Choir and congregation were sprinkled with bits and pieces of professional bands and quartets from just about every group on the Opry. Friday and Saturday nights they entertained the fans in the Opry House. Sunday they praised the Lord at Evangel Temple.

At the same time gospel music was climbing the record charts. Performers, writers, promoters, deejays, recording companies, and broadcast executives were all getting on the bandwagon to satisfy public demand.

I felt Evangel Tempel should have a gospel broadcast. What better way to extend the ministry of the church? Friends suggested I talk to WSM, owned by the National Life and Accident Insurance Company, which was also the parent corporation of the Grand Ole Opry.

WSM Radio had been the bellwether of country music stations for almost half a century, blanketing most of the United States and Canada with 50,000 watts on a clear channel. WSM's Channel 4 Television had one of the largest viewing audiences in the upper mid-south.

Because so many preachers wanted air time, WSM had a policy of not selling time to anybody. Instead they gave time on a rotating basis to the larger churches. Evangel Temple didn't have one tenth the membership of, say, First Baptist Church, but it had many country music personalities related to the WSM corporate family. And a pastor who was sort of an unofcial chaplain for Grand Ole Opry people.

"Come up with a format," they said, "and maybe we can give you a half hour of TV time on Sunday morning at eight."

"Gospel Country" was a low key, soft sell combination of entertainment and inspiration, featuring the biggest names in country music as guest artists. I emceed the show and did trio arrangements with Carol and Larry King, backed by a six-man band. Between numbers I ad-libbed Scripture, read poems, gave an occasional testimony, and invited viewers to visit Evangel Temple.

While the air time was free, we had to pay union scale for stagehands, band members, and musicians. This ran to about $500 a week, almost as much as we were taking in at the church. Members and friends of the church pledged the extra amount. Some who benefited from the union rule gave back part of their wages.

It was well worth all the sacrifice. The viewer index rose until "Gospel Country" was rated one of the top religious telecasts and second among all TV programs in the Nashville area.

Part of the agreement with the station was that we would use Opry talent as guest artists. I knew the Opry performers were a mixed bag religiously, ranging from Sunday school teachers to some who never attended church. But even if we hadn't had the agreement with the station, I wouldn't have tried to check spiritual barometers anyway. Anyone familiar with the Nashville music scene knows that some of the biggest hypocrites are "gospel" singers while some of the finest Christians are just entertainers. I don't mean to infer that all gospel musicians are hypocrites. Certainly not the Rambos, the Spears, the Hemphills, and a number of others. But there are also those who will give a gospel concert, then head for a motel with a bottle and a girl. The title "gospel" doesn't necessarily mean a thing.

We rehearsed and taped "Gospel Country" on Wednesday

evening before a live studio audience. I tried to keep every-body relaxed and the pressure down. I also kept a lookout for performers with obvious spiritual needs.

For one of the early shows we had Connie Smith, who a couple of years before had been voted female vocalist of the year. Connie, a beautiful honey blonde and just twenty-six, was already into her second rocky marriage.

She sang "In the Garden" then sat down out of camera range on the far side of the studio. Near the end of the show I noticed her crying. After signing off, I walked over and asked if I could be of any help.

"I don't know why I'm crying," she said.

"Maybe God is speaking to you," I ventured.

Then she began telling me about her family problems.

I opened my little New Testament and read verses about Jesus' sacrificial death on the cross.

The tears kept trickling down her face, smudging her makeup, as she listened attentively.

"Connie, would you like to pray the sinner's prayer and ask Jesus to come into your heart?"

"Yes," she murmured softly.

She lifted her hands and prayed out loud while the camera-men, band, and studio audience looked on.

"Do you believe His promises are true, Connie? Has He saved you?"

"Oh, yes. I know it."

"Praise God. Then thank Him right here."

And she did.

Connie became a member of Evangel Temple. Her husband attended only a few times. Their marriage situation didn't improve, but Connie had peace that God was with her.

She gave her testimony from the Opry stage and became a one-woman dynamo for the Lord. She brought some of the biggest stars in country music to the services. Many of them went to the altar to receive Christ. Connie also took a 30,000 mile benefit tour of the Far East for the children of Bangladesh, witnessing for Christ wherever she sang. "Even if I knew there wasn't a heaven or hell, the Lord has given me such peace and joy, I'd still want to be a Christian," she told audiences from Australia to Japan.

From '67 to '72 Evangel Tempel grew like wildfire. Jeannie C. Riley of "Harper Valley P.T.A." fame prayed at our altar. Barbara Fairchild, who lived in St. Louis at the time, visited Nashville, and was saved in the services. Bill Mack, a big-time country music deejay from Fort Worth, recommitted his life to Christ. So far as I know they are still living for the Lord. There were other stars, whose names I won't mention, who made commitments but later apparently fell by the wayside.

We reached many more people from other segments of the music industry. Larry Gatlin who would become one of the best-known song writers in Nashville began coming. Barbara Miller and her daughter Pam were saved when we were meeting in the basement. Later Barbara's husband, Eddy, was converted. Eddy and Pam wrote several gospel songs, which Connie Smith recorded, based on sermons I preached. "Crumbs from the Table" was inspired by a message on the rich man and Lazarus. "The Last Altar Call" came from my style of giving an evangelistic invitation.

Eddy is probably best known for writing "Please Release Me." After he found Christ, he wrote, "Please Release Me from My Sins."

Some who came to Christ during this period were old friends from many years back. Elaine Tubb's father, Ernest, had helped dad get on the Opry. She and I had knocked around together as kids backstage. Now she was grown up and married to song writer Wayne Walker. Their son came to Vacation Bible School at the church and Elaine was saved at the graduation exercises.

Dottie Lee was another well-known person in the music community. Her parents, Dottie and Smokey Swan, had come to the Opry before dad. As a cherubic, golden-haired little girl Dottie had closed the Eddie Arnold show singing "God Bless America." Later she and I had been on a tour together when she was twelve and I was sixteen. Her mother and dad, and Wilma Lee and Stoney had been long time friends since the Wheeling, West Virginia days. I saw her at the Opry and while talking about old times invited her to Evangel Temple. She and her husband Larry both came and were saved.

More recently Dottie had been helping with the TV program and teaching Carol the art of backup singing for soloists on the Opry and in recording sessions. I was glad to see Carol and Dottie become good friends, for, since leaving evangelistic work, I had been extremely busy with the church and had neglected Carol. I figured that if Carol developed more interests outside the home, she would be less dependent on me. Besides, we needed the extra money she earned singing.

We decided to drop the TV show in 1970. Some of the church members felt the cost was too much of a burden. I didn't want to cause a rift and agreed to stop the program.

I continued to stay in touch with friends in the music community. John Cash was one who had always been friendly to me, although I didn't know him well. "John," as friends and family knew him, was now married to June Carter, the daughter of my old friends, E. J. and Maybelle Carter. I had heard that John was trying hard to stay off pills and alcohol and live for God, and I wanted to be of any help that I could.

Nashville had long buzzed with Johnny Cash stories. A couple I could appreciate were about motels. In one instance he and his sidemen reportedly painted their rooms jet black, then checked out. Another time they supposedly moved the beds and furniture into the hall and called the room clerk. He arrived to find four grown men apparently asleep and ran back to the manager. When the manager got there they had moved the furniture back into the rooms, leaving the clerk standing agape trying to explain what had happened.

Larry and Dottie also got to be good friends with John's guitarist, Luther Perkins. Luther's tragic death in a house fire shocked everyone. And because of their common friendship with Luther, the Lees asked John to come to the church and sing a few songs in his memory. The "Man in Black" was glad to oblige.

John had now formed his own music publishing company. His House of Cash employed two of Evangel Temple's most active and enthusiastic members. Larry Lee was his office manager, and Dottie Lee was the company receptionist. John could hardly avoid hearing about Evangel Temple, and was friendly, but he made no move to come and hear me preach.

Because we had once run on parallel tracks I felt an affinity with John. I went down to watch tapings of his new ABC-TV series a few times. I didn't pester him about coming to church, but just talked and shared a few jokes.

Meanwhile, his sister Joanne arrived from Houston and began working at his House of Cash. Dottie began witnessing to her right away and things began happening. When Joanne gave her testimony at the church goose bumps ran up my spine.

"I had just come off a horrible divorce," she said. "I was drinking and on drugs and if it hadn't been for my children I might have committed suicide. In this depression I called John and he said, 'Come on home to me, I love you and I want you.' The sweetest words I'd ever heard. I drove all the way from Houston, so stoned I couldn't remember the trip, and my three kids were with me.

"John gave me a job. I walked into the company and there was this beautiful, smiling blonde at the reception desk. Day by day, Dottie witnessed to me, telling me there was hope in

Jesus. 'Yeah, yeah, yeah,' I said to myself. I didn't believe it. Finally I told her, 'Look, Dottie, just skip it, there's no hope for me. I'm too bad.'

" 'Wait a minute, girl,' she shot back, and began laying the truth on me that Jesus had died for the worst of sinners. A spark started in my heart. A tiny, tiny spark. But the devil tried to quench it. I was afraid it wasn't real.

"The Cash family has a reunion in Arkansas every October. John rented a six-seater plane to fly us over that Saturday. After the dinner on the ground we started back. The sky got dark. I had always been scared to fly and now I really got frightened.

"The cloud got blacker and bigger. It started raining, then hailing. John knew I was scared to death and kept looking back and making the okay sign with his thumb and finger. I put my head in my lap and started to pray. Suddenly I heard somebody scream. Then I realized it was me screaming, 'Jesus, help me!'

"I thought we were going to crash but after a little while, the air got smooth. All the while I was praying, 'Jesus, if you'll get us home safely, I'll call Dottie and go to church with her.' I really felt it was my last chance.

"When we landed, I called Dottie and told her, 'I'm going to your church with you tomorrow.' When I walked through those big doors, the Spirit of God almost knocked me back. I ran and jumped in my car and drove home.

"The next week was the most miserable time of my life. On Sunday morning I came back and went all the way up to the second row. I call that the 'Glory Row' now, 'cause that's where God gave me His glory. When you gave the invitation, Brother Snow, I was the first one down. I prayed for two hours. It took that long, not for Jesus to save me, but for me to accept that He really did love me."

When Joanne got through everybody in the church was bawling and praising the Lord.

Joanne also brought the next member of the Cash family to church, twelve-year-old Rosey, June Carter Cash's daughter from a previous marriage. Rose was saved and began working on the others.

I knew John was going through some deep water but I didn't press him. The details of his struggle in coming back to God are told in his autobiography *Man in Black.* I'll mention only some of the instances that relate directly to me and Evangel Temple.

Late one afternoon he phoned and asked if I would like to see his place of private worship. By the time I got to his house it was dark.

We jumped in his jeep and blazed a trail to a little frame cabin in the woods. We got out and stood there in the damp weeds before it.

"Would you dedicate my little church to the Lord, Jimmy?" he requested.

I asked God to set apart the little cabin for meditation and worship. John followed with a simple petition for strength and guidance. He would later tell me that he was deathly afraid of snakes and that was the first thing he thought about while standing there in sandals. Then as we prayed, he just totally forgot about the snakes.

We stood there maybe half an hour in the darkness, praying and talking. I suggested that it was good to get alone with God, but that he shouldn't shut his Christian experience off from the world. I encouraged him to take his whole family to church, if not Evangel Temple, then somewhere else where he could have Christian fellowship and feed on the Word of God.

A week or so after that John started bringing his whole family to Evangel Temple regularly. One Sunday morning he heard me preach from Acts 16:31, "Believe on the Lord Jesus Christ and thou shalt be saved and thy house," and emphasize that a father should lead his family in faith.

John came down to the altar and said, "Jimmy, I've decided if my whole house is going to be together, I need to be the first one to step out publicly."

June and the children followed.

John Cash gave Evangel Temple an added burst of fame. We had problems with fans and were forced to post a sign asking visitors not to take pictures or ask for autographs inside the church. We also had to be very careful about special music, because so many aspiring artists wanted to sing before John and the other stars in the church.

But we didn't want to turn people away. Almost every Sunday somebody came to see the celebrities and went away praising God for salvation. But we didn't want John, June, Connie Smith, and others to be disturbed in Bible study and worship either.

It would have taken a secret service detail to keep people away from John. He was there every time the doors opened and frequently went to the altar to pray with people. One Sunday he followed a fellow down and knelt beside him. The guy whipped out a sheet of music, and whispered, "Hey Johnny, I've written this song that I know will be a hit. Give a listen."

John cut him off kindly. "Brother, I don't think this is quite the place. If you'll call my office in the morning, my secretary will set up an appointment."

So far as I know, John talked to the song writer. That's the kind of man he is.

John was always inviting people to the services. One of his friends who came was Glen Sherley. John had met Sherley when giving a concert at California's Folsom Prison. He sang a song Glen had written and helped to get his release.

Glen had been on drugs real bad. He used to shoot up heroin with a football needle and always wore a long sleeve shirt to cover the big bumps that covered both arms.

John was in New York City when he heard Glen was coming to Evangel Temple. He hopped a plane and flew back just to be with him. They went to the altar together and after Glen turned his life over to Jesus, John flew back to the East Coast.

John Cash was the kind of layman every pastor likes to have

in his church, the kind who will praise you for stepping on his toes, and pray for you instead of cutting you down.

John knew the church was having some internal problems during the summer of 1971. There were misunderstandings and hurt feelings between certain key members. He sensed that I didn't quite know what to do.

He took my Bible and wrote on the flyleaf a personal prayer:

Dear God:

Please fill Jimmy Snow with wisdom. Make him to grow daily in spiritual strength. Anoint him with your Holy Spirit each time he stands to preach your truth. May soul winning through him be multiplied from this day. Protect him from "little people." May his church be a mighty fortress for right. May its membership multiply. May it be a lighthouse and may Jimmy Snow reflect your light. May the fullness of understanding of your Word be his that it is always in his heart and mind, to be instantly on his tongue. May he lift and inspire men by the thousands as he has myself.

Amen. Johnny Cash

The Lord answered John's prayer. The church kept growing.

A couple of months later John asked me for help. "I've decided to do a film. A testimony of how I feel about Jesus in song and narration."

I couldn't imagine what he had in mind. But I'd learned to pay attention to John Cash. He may not have much formal education, but he's one of the most intelligent man I've ever known.

"June is going to work with me. You know she had two years of dramatic training in New York. We'll go to Israel and film on location. Walk the gospel road. Climb the mountain where Jesus was tempted by the devil. Follow His footsteps up Calvary's hill. Try to recapture the way it was when He was on earth."

"Do you have a screenplay?"

John laughed. "A sponsor lost interest when I told him I didn't want a network's approval in advance. I want this film to express the way we feel when we're doing it."

"What do you want with me? I'm no actor."

"You can be my literary consultant. Tell me when I'm going off the deep end. Will you do it?"

I didn't have to think twice before saying yes.

We flew to the Holy Land in October and spent a month in the field. As on previous trips to the land of the Bible I was fascinated by the sights and the people. I could have stayed a year.

John narrated and sang the "old, old story" as it touched his soul. Bob Elfstrom, the director, played Jesus. The rest of us in the troupe of thirty took minor roles—I was Pilate—and local hired talent completed the cast. One of our guides, an Arab who spoke fluent English, even got in the film as a Pharisee.

Assad, the guide, knew Bible history better than any of us but God wasn't real to him. By his own admission he was a cheat and a sharpie. A married man, he bragged about affairs with other women and about how he got good tips from American "pilgrims." "I let the holy rollers baptize me in the Spirit and the Baptists dunk me in the Jordan. I oughta be clean by now, heh?" he laughed.

"No," I told him. "You aren't clean until you repent and ask Jesus to wash your sins away. If you don't you'll stand before God in judgment and be condemned."

He just laughed. But he was a good guide.

We came home in November with twenty-two hours of film that would have to be edited down to ninety minutes. With some contemporary scenes to be shot in New York and Las Vegas and spliced in, the work was just beginning.

A capacity crowd at the church welcomed us back and "amened" our testimonies. The murmuring and complaining seemed to have quieted down. The altar was full that Sunday morning.

Sunday services were now packed out and we were putting chairs in the aisle. "We've got to do something about this," John declared. "I'll talk to the man who built my home."

Buoyed by John's enthusiasm, the church accepted the builder's plan to extend the sanctuary and double the seating capacity to five hundred. Some extra touches were a sixty-four bulb chandelier to hang below a center skylight—the "Resurrection Hole"—and two massive, ornate doors from the old Harris County Courthouse in Houston, Texas.

During the month away and while the church was being enlarged I had been doing a lot of thinking and praying. Before going to Israel with John, I had been having some family problems and was now worried they were getting worse. I had an intuition that things had been going too well at the church. I sensed that the devil had been lying back awaiting an opportunity to discredit my ministry.

To prepare the people for what I felt was coming, I began a series of sixteen sermons on Satan, his origin, goals, methods, wiles. Everything I could find in Scripture about the nature and strategy of the deceiver and enemy of God. I wanted to expose him for what he was.

"This may cost me dearly," I said in beginning the first sermon. "I expect Satan to fight me all the way."

I never dreamed then how hard he would fight or how great would be the cost.

12
Feet of Clay

Since 1972 the Nashville gossip vultures have had a feast. On me.

They're still picking the bones and probably will be twenty years from now.

"I knew it all along."

"That Jimmy Snow is a disgrace to Christianity."

"If there's any kind of preacher's court, they ought to boot him out of the ministry."

And from some of my former members, "We love Brother Snow. God has used him. But—"

"It's a shame what has happened to Brother Snow."

Perhaps the unkindest cut of all came in a magazine article published by one of the big denominations that has its main publishing headquarters in Nashville. The article told about the conversion of Connie Smith. All the principals were named except the one who led her to Christ. I was simply "the pastor of Evangel Temple." It was as if the name Jimmy Snow was poison.

These next two chapters will tell how a preacher can fall from the top of the ladder to rock bottom. I tell it not to justify myself, although some will see it that way, but to bring a ray of hope to those bearing the stigma of failure, those who fear their mistakes have closed the door of useful service to God forever.

I knew that many preachers' marriages were not heaven and honey long before Carol and I began having problems. I heard it from their teenage kids during revivals and I saw it firsthand in the way some pastoral couples got along in the parsonage. One pastor confessed to me that he and his wife hadn't had marital relations in months, adding, "But I've got to pretend everything's all right, or I'm in trouble with the church." A preacher's marriage was supposed to be perfect and he felt he had to play that role.

Team marriages where preacher and wife worked together in the Lord's vineyard seemed to work best. Glen and Helen Miller were an inspiration. He was the pastor and she the choir director, but there wasn't a smidgen of jealousy between them. The little affections and courtesies they cast at each other while we were relaxing after the services were beautiful.

I felt Carol and I were a team like the Millers.

Young people saw us that way and were impressed. As one starry-eyed couple put it after a campfire service, "We want our marriage to be like yours."

I never thought it would be otherwise. Even after we left evangelism, we continued as a team with Carol playing the organ and leading the choir. More than anyone else, it was Carol who built the Evangel Temple choir that visitors raved over.

In January, 1969, the U.S. State Department sent Carol and me and two supporting singers to entertain the troops in Vietnam. We had made a shorter tour with dad three years before. Flying in fast moving Huey battle copters, often skimming the treetops to spoil the aim of enemy gunners, we did fifty-one performances in six weeks.

We had some frightening moments.

When we arrived at one camp just behind the front lines, the officer in charge warned, "These guys are pretty keyed up. I can't guarantee how your show will go. They threw bottles at the last performers. If they start that, get off the stage immediately."

The boys came right in from the battlefield and sat on bleachers with cases of beer and whiskey stuck between their legs. At the start they were noisy and profane, but ten minutes into the show they fell stone quiet. When we finished many were weeping.

At Long Bien we were in the middle of the show when Communist sappers broke through the fence. The stands emptied in ten seconds. We dropped our instruments, ran and dove into a ditch.

We saw the horrors of war close up. Eighteen and nineteen-year-olds in hospitals with their faces blown off. Hard-eyed infantrymen carrying enemy ears on their belts. "Why?" I asked one. "When you find your friends skinned alive and their organs sewed in their mouths, you start playing the Communists' game," he said.

We spent one night in a CIA villa and heard enemy prisoners being tortured in the next room. We were told that a favorite way to make a prisoner talk was to take him and a friend up in a helicopter, shove the friend out, and say, "You're next, if you don't tell us what we want to know."

When we questioned such inhumanities they told us about how the Communists taught six-year-olds to hide hand grenades under their clothing and pull the pin when American soldiers walked by.

Carol and I went through all this together.

Through 1969 I felt we had a good marriage. About the only time we fussed was when we were getting ready to go somewhere.

Taking after dad, I kept my clothes in perfect order, suits on one side of the closet, sports clothes in the center, dress shirts on the other side, and shoes shined and lined up on the floor. The only difference was my shoes pointed in while his pointed out. Just like dad, I wore my clothes by rotation, even down to socks and underwear, and never had to decide what I was going to wear on a particular day.

Carol was a little less orderly.

I would be dressed and ready to go to church on time while she seemed to always be a little late getting herself and Vanessa ready. I would sit and fume and look at my watch in frustration, another propensity I got from dad.

After church it was the reverse. She would be ready to leave while I wanted to stay around and talk.

Our solution was to get a second car. Now we could each go to church and leave at our own convenience. This was a mistake, but I didn't realize it at the time.

Something else I didn't see was that I was putting the church ahead of my family, way ahead. I thought I had to be in charge of every meeting and spend time with every person who wanted to see me.

Occasionally Carol asked me, "Why do you give a stranger your undivided attention as long as they want to talk, and then come home and cut your family short?" I would ask myself, "Why don't I listen to Carol as I do someone else?"

"Because I want to be a good pastor," I assured myself.

I didn't perceive that there were times when being a good husband should take precedence over pastoral duties.

What I did see was Carol withdrawing more and more. My answer was another stop-gap solution: "Find some friends you enjoy being with. They'll keep you from being lonesome when I'm busy."

She took my advice. She went horseback riding, shopping, and all around town with them.

The pressure eased. I felt good. She had her world. I had

mine. And we could still work together in the church.

I didn't feel good for long though. I'd come home and find she was out with her friends. She wasn't available when I wanted her. She stayed out later than I thought she should.

We argued bitterly.

Who does a preacher talk to when his marriage is falling apart? He can't go to his members as they go to him. He's ashamed to talk to another pastor. He's afraid he will be seen going to a professional marriage counselor.

That was me, when my church was the fastest growing congregation in my denomination.

I didn't talk to a soul until it was too late. Nobody at the church knew that Carol and I were physically separated at home. They only saw us up front Sunday morning, both smiling.

Carol was now expecting our second child. But there was no joy in our house. Instead, tension was up. She complained that I was never home, and didn't have any interest in my family. She was just a fixture. I cared more for the church members and my friends at the House of Cash than for her.

I threw the words back at her and stomped out of the house. After driving around for a while, I cooled down enough to see her side better. Lately I had been either at the church or at the House of Cash from morning until night, sometimes late at night, seven days a week. I had been going to lunch with friends at the House of Cash—Joanne Cash, Larry and Dottie Lee, both members of our church, and others who were working on the *Gospel Road* film. We talked about the film, the church, and some of their problems.

Carol and I just seemed to talk past each other. A breakdown in communication, the professionals call it.

I would come home and find a note. I would wait up for her, pace the floor, try to concentrate on TV, anything to pass the time, then at the sound of a car run and peek out the bathroom window. If it was her car I would run and jump in bed and pretend to be asleep. Pride wouldn't let me admit that I wanted her home so badly.

Then came the nights when I didn't look out the bathroom window. I slept in the den, or on the couch in my office at the church, being careful to go home before any of the staff showed up.

Shannon Lee was born December 29, 1971. Carol's friends took her to the hospital. I showed up only a couple of times. I was a coward. I felt the split-up was coming. I didn't want to get too attached to the baby. The thought of losing Carol and Vanessa was hard enough to bear.

In midsummer, 1972, we went to Las Vegas with John and June Cash to finish up filming for *The Gospel Road*. I hoped the trip might help our relationship, but nothing changed. Except for, "You can use the bathroom now," we had very little to say to one another.

A few months after our trip to Vegas I flew to Los Angeles for a visit with Pat Boone. Pat is from Nashville and married to one of Red Foley's daughters. He and Shirley had been close to a breakup before God got hold of their lives. I envied their radiant happiness.

They had some Hollywood friends in for a small party one night; actually it was more a prayer and praise service. The actress Joanna Moore came and told how she had been messed up with drugs and alcohol and had lost her daughter Tatum to her ex-husband Ryan O'Neal at their divorce. "I got saved too late to save my marriage," she said in essence. "I can't change the past. But I know God's forgiven me and has something meaningful for me to do."

It hurt to know that my marriage was breaking up too.

I asked Joanna to come to Nashville and share her testimony. "You can help people who have gone through a similar experience," I said. She did come later.

I went home. It was still the same with Carol and me. I wondered how long we could keep pretending before the church.

Carol took the first step in ending the charade. She began to slip out of church after playing the organ to await the end of the service in the office. She only returned to play for the altar call.

The first two times it happened I didn't say anything, and I hoped no one else in the church had paid any attention. Sometimes she never reappeared at all, though, and finally I had to ask a friend, Mrs. Dewey, to cover for Carol at the organ.

One Saturday afternoon in August I was conducting a wedding. Carol was at the organ. She played the prelude and the march, but, about half way through the ceremony, she left the organ bench, took Vanessa by the hand and walked out. It was the last time she was in Evangel Temple.

The next morning Mrs. Dewey was at the organ and directed the choir. I knew I had to tell the congregation now. Just before the benediction, I announced, "Carol and I are having problems. You'd better prepare for the worst. We're separated."

There was a shocked hush. The congregation sat stunned. After the benediction they slipped out quietly and stood in the parking lot talking in small groups.

I had been dropping little hints to Vanessa, and I suppose Carol had, too, that something was going to happen. A few days prior, I had called her aside. I put my arm around her and drew her close. Only ten, she looked so small and unprotected.

"Honey, you know your mother and I haven't been getting along," I said huskily. She bobbed her head, fighting to hold back the tears.

"Parents aren't perfect. They make mistakes. I know I've made my share. I haven't spent as much time with you and your mom as I should. But we can't go back and change the past."

She was crying now. I muddled on for a few minutes, being careful not to blame Carol.

"We'll probably split. If we do, we want you to know that you aren't at fault in any way. And that no matter what happens we both love you."

I just had to get out of town for a few days. I guess God had it all planned. I had to go to Canada to preach in a week's youth camp, an engagement made over a year before that I couldn't cancel. I was hurting, really hurting. "Lord help me," I must have prayed a thousand times. The show had to go on.

During that week I tried to analyze our miserable situation. Carol and I couldn't seem to get things together. The church was in turmoil. Our parents were upset and didn't know what to do about us. Vanessa was torn, not knowing what would happen next. What would be the end of it all?

I reached a decision. When I landed back in Nashville the following Monday, I went immediately to the courthouse and filed for divorce. Rash as it may sound, I hoped this action might shake up Carol and cause her to seek a reconciliation.

The church board called us both to an emergency meeting. Appearing separately, each of us said we wanted to save our marriage.

The week rocked along. We were still living in the house, though in the comings and goings we were passing like ships in the night.

Friday night I went to church for an all night prayer meeting. I returned home Saturday morning to find the house stripped. Everything was gone except my personal belongings.

In one way it was a relief. In another, a hammer blow. I fell to the bare floor crying. Except for the night at the mailbox, I think I wept the hardest of any time in my life.

It wasn't just the ripping apart of a marriage. It was the breakup of a team that God had used mightily.

The rest of that day was a blur. How long I stayed on my face I don't know. How I managed to preach two sermons on Sunday I don't know.

The next week I had a talk with my lawyer. He said Carol had cross-filed. When I told him I wanted her to have custody of the children, he advised that I withdraw my suit. "It'll be easier to reach an agreement if you'll let the record show that she took the initiative." I consented. I didn't want a fight.

A meeting was set up between us. We agreed on a financial settlement. Carol would get the furniture and $10,000 for her part in the house, which I would borrow. I would also pay $200 a month child support.

The news of the breakup of the pastor of the most publicized church in town hit Nashville like a hurricane. The story was splashed across the newspapers and reported on TV and radio newscasts. Paul Harvey took note on his national telecast: "Ex-country music entertainer and preacher Jimmy Snow and wife Carol are divorcing." The fan magazines made us a gossip tidbit.

The wildest story was headlined in a Texas newspaper which quoted me as saying from the pulpit that the Lord had told me to divorce Carol and marry another woman in the congregation.

The months before the divorce became final were the worst. About fifty people left the church. Accusations flew on both sides. Private detectives were hired.

I can say nothing about Carol, but I must mention an item on the Nashville police record about me. Coming back from a dinner engagement with six friends, I stopped at Dottie Lee's house to use the telephone. Her two grown sons and two younger children were there. While I was inside two policemen knocked on the door and arrested me on a charge of illegal cohabitation. The policemen apologized and said that anyone can go down to the station, make charges against someone, and have them arrested. The charge was dismissed in court, but it added a lot of fuel to the gossip.

I did take one sensible action. The Saturday after Carol

moved out, I had a couple of single fellows from the church move in with me. A friend gave us some beds to sleep on.

But there was nothing I could do to stop the ugly gossip. I was made out to be the biggest playboy in town with half a dozen women on the string. It was ridiculous. When I wasn't at the church, I was with friends and never alone with a single woman.

The battle had spread far beyond Carol and me by this time. People were choosing sides.

At a conference with our respective lawyers, we drew up an agreement not to say anything derogatory about each other and to encourage our friends to do the same. I was concerned for the church so I readily agreed. As long as people were talking about me, the church would suffer.

The lawyers drew up the agreement and we signed.

After that when people asked me about who was at fault, I responded as I did to John Pugh, a writer for *Nashville!* magazine, "In our divorce agreement there was a stipulation that neither party would say anything damaging about the other. Next question."

Being a well-known pastor, I was assumed to be guilty. When the divorce became final another forty or fifty left the church, some because they assumed the worst of me.

There was now an active movement to get my ordination revoked so I could not continue to pastor an Assembly of God Church. Dissenters reported me to the district superintendent who asked me to come for a confidential conference. After we talked, he stated that the divorce was not grounds for expulsion, but that if I remarried my ministerial standing would be automatically terminated.

That didn't stop the troublemakers. They accused me of claiming to see visions in the services and preaching false doctrine. Fortunately, all of my sermons were on tape and available for anyone to check.

Pressure continued mounting for me to resign. Several good friends advised that it would be better for all concerned if I would leave. I promised to pray about it. I assured them that I, too, felt the future of the church was more important than my reputation.

A preacher friend suggested I go to another state and start a new church.

I wrestled with the Lord in prayer. I couldn't get peace to leave.

I did advise the celebrities in the church that it might be best for them to leave. "Of course, I want you to stay," I said. "But you could be more embarrassed by further association with me."

Several left. Connie Smith, who had just gone through an agonizing divorce, stayed on for a while. And John Cash, God bless him, gave his opinion when TV talk show host Stanley Siegel asked him why he continued to attend Evangel Temple "when you know all these stories about your pastor." Said John, "I know what I feel when I go there."

Siegel had me on the following week. I didn't dare not go. Absence would imply admission of guilt.

He invited people to call the studio and talk with me. Most of the calls were accusations. "What scriptural basis do you have for getting a divorce?" "What right do you have to stand in the pulpit and tell other people how to live?" Things like that. I recognized some of the callers as people who had left the church.

I could only say I believed God had forgiven me of any mistakes I had made, and that I had a clear conscience and just wanted to keep serving God at Evangel Temple so long as the congregation would let me.

I went through a period of feeling sorry for myself and questioning God. "Lord, I have lost my wife and children, and am judged guilty for things I have not done. Now I may lose my church and every bit of influence I have in Nashville. Oh, Lord, when there are so many great things I could be doing for you, what have I done to deserve this?

"Lord, all I know is show business and preaching. If I can't preach, how can I make it as an entertainer? If I can't work, how will I keep up the child-support payments?

"Lord, why did you call me to preach in the first place, if you were going to allow this to happen?

"Lord, where are you? Where's your power? What possible good can come out of this mess?

"Lord, why, why, why?"

I still hadn't opened my heart to anyone. All I had to show for my isolation was a painful ulcer.

One preacher kept coming to mind—Charles Greenaway, a former missionary to lepers in Africa. A man who had been healed of blackwater fever. He had been a good friend during the year Carol and I had spent in Springfield, Missouri.

Later on, in May 1973 Charles came to Nashville and preached for me. He listened as I unburdened my heart to him. Then he said, "Jimmy, I had a preacher friend whom God called to visit in TB hospitals and pray for the patients. God performed fantastic miracles. Many were saved and healed. Then he came down with TB himself and died. And his wife wondered why."

Charlie sighed. "How many divorces have there been in the church this year?"

I counted on my fingers. "Let's see. Connie Smith was the first. When mine is final, there'll be nine. In the previous six years, we've only had four."

"You've spent a lot of time counseling, I suppose?"

"Man, those are just the ones that went to court. Marriage trouble is a disease in this music community. I wish I had a dollar for every hour I've listened to marriage problems. If I'd spent half the time with Carol I spent listening to other women, we might be together now. But it's too late."

"Don't you see what happened, Jimmy? You caught the disease. You've become a victim of the disease of those you were trying to help. Just like the preacher in the TB hospitals."

He paused, then asked, "Do you feel the price is too great?"

"If you put it that way, no. But I never thought it would cost me so much."

After talking with Charles Greenaway, I knew I couldn't go back on the Lord. But I was still unsettled about the church. One day I was ready to resign—the next determined to stay.

The pressure remained. Some members were saying, "We're going to wait a little longer. If you get married again, that's the end."

They were threatening me about something I hadn't seriously considered. I decided that no matter what I did, the noose would remain around my neck. There was just one way out: resign. Maybe some churches would invite me to preach on Sunday. But as a pastor, I was finished.

In October I wrote out my resignation at the house, slipped it in an envelope and took it to the church. It was on my desk. I was going to read it to the people that Sunday.

Brenda Crawford, the church secretary, came in and asked to borrow an envelope. Absent-mindedly I gave her the one with my resignation in it.

Brenda was good friends with everybody. Some of the former members of our church had tried to get her to leave, but she had stuck. "I believe this is where God wants me," she said, "and until He moves me out, this is where I'm going to stay."

She handed the resignation back to me. "Throw it in the trash. You won't be needing that." And she walked out.

I left a little later, slamming the door.

When I came back and sat down at the desk, I noticed a poster picture had been taped on the back of the office door. It showed a young football player, sitting on the bench with head bowed and helmet hanging loosely from his hands. The big caption underneath read: I QUIT.

There was a smaller picture at the bottom. Three crosses on a hill. I got up and walked around the desk to read the smaller print underneath the middle cross: I DIDN'T.

Brenda dropped in a few minutes later and found me sitting there before the picture weeping my head off. All she did was grin and say, "You're not going anywhere, are you?"

I wiped my eyes. "No. I guess not."

13
I Cannot Go Back

After Brenda returned to her office a new wave of self-pity hit me.

Where had I failed, except to put God's work ahead of my family? "Cruel and inhumane treatment," the divorce charge read.

Why had I done this? To minister to others. To do what I felt was expected in the ministry.

Now my marriage was over the brink. I was a scandal to those I had led to Christ.

"Why, Lord? Why? It isn't fair."

The answer finally came in the small hours of the night.

"So that I might get the glory. You were riding high. You were the big wheel. The preacher everybody was bragging about. The one numbered among the celebrities. Now I'm getting the glory. People are looking to Me, not Jimmy Snow. They're coming to Evangel Temple because of Me."

I looked again at the caption under the middle cross at the bottom of the poster: I DIDN'T.

The Lord hadn't quit. Not when He was tempted by the devil in the wilderness. Not when He was falsely accused. Not when He hung on that cross. And He was the purest one who ever lived.

I searched the Scriptures for a text that expressed my determination and found Jephthah's words in Judges 11:35: ". . . I have opened my mouth unto the Lord, and *I cannot go back*" (italics mine).

On Sunday evening I read the text to the church. "The old devil has tempted me to give up and throw in the towel," I said in a breaking voice. "He has whispered in my ear, 'What have you got for fourteen years of serving God? Nothing.' I can only answer this morning in the words of Jephthah: 'I cannot go back . . . I cannot go back.'

"I've felt Satan's vise grip my soul until I've wanted to run as hard and as far as I could go. The tears have flowed like a river. My heart and mind have been pounded. But I cannot go back. I cannot go back. I love the Lord too much. I've been through too much. I cannot go back."

It was the 29th of October, 1972. My coat and tie were off, my collar unbuttoned, and the perspiration was rolling down my face. There was no smoothness in my delivery as I cited others who vowed to serve the Lord and suffered.

Daniel, thrown into the den of lions. The Hebrew children, shoved into the fiery furnace. Peter, according to tradition, crucified upside down. Stephen, stoned to death.

Thousands of first-century Christians fed to ravenous lions in the Roman sports arena. John Bunyan, rotting in jail.

"They paid the price because they could not go back."

It was a long sermon, almost an hour and a half, of confession and rededication to my vows made that night at the mailbox.

"I've failed God. You're going to fail Him too. Don't let it get you down. Pick yourself back up and stand for Jesus. Refuse to give in to the devil.

"Will you join me as I promise to the best of my ability to be what God wants me to be?

"It's time to say as Moses did, 'Let those who are on the Lord's side, stand. . . .'

"There's no valley that God cannot give us strength to walk through, for if God be for us, who can be against us?"

I gave the altar call for the renewing of vows. I was down there with others, sobbing, "Lord, I cannot go back. I cannot go back. Help me go forward."

Then leading out we sang the song, "It will be worth it all, when we see Jesus. . . ."

Through the fall and spring, I believe I did the best preaching of my life. Not by the world's standards, but by God's. More souls were saved than in any previous six-month period in the history of the church. To God be the glory.

I was preaching both to myself and the congregation.

From Scripture I shared encouragement from others who had failed God and come back, notably Peter.

"Peter, the leader of the apostles, cursed and denied the Lord three times on the eve of Calvary. When the rooster crowed he realized his guilt and repented in bitter tears. God was not finished with Peter. God had something else for him to do. He became the Spirit-filled preacher of Pentecost

"Peter didn't crawl in a hole to die. He refused to yield to the cold wind of unforgiving spirits. He went forth anew to serve a merciful, loving God.

"If Peter could go forward, I can. And this church can. Amen? Amen."

There was no audible voice from heaven, no vision. But the command to my soul was unmistakable: "Go forward. Give me the glory, and I will be with you."

Earlier in the year I had felt God wanted us to get back into broadcasting. My idea was to tape a weekly radio program at the church for broadcast over WSM's 50,000 watt Opry station. We would use Opry talent as we had on the TV show and I would preach a short sermon. By recording it at the church the cost would be minimal.

When I outlined the format to Bud Wendell, then the supervisor of the Opry, he suggested doing it live after the Friday night Opry. I had never thought this would be possible, since the Opry management tried to maintain a strict neutrality in religion. I gulped and said I was agreeable.

"Good, good," he beamed. "When can you start?"

"Two weeks," I ventured.

The air time would be free. But we'd have to pay the stage workers and performers union scale. It would run about what the TV expense had, around $500 a week. Money the church didn't have.

I put the opportunity before the people of ministering to a different crowd of Opry fans every Friday night and broadcasting to over forty states and Canada. Sixty-eight pledged support above their regular church gifts to the new "Grand Ole Gospel Time."

The next two weeks were hectic. We prayed around the clock one night. On the Friday evening of the first broadcast the choir rehearsed at the church, then all of us took the familiar route downtown to the old red-brick Ryman Auditorium which had housed the Opry since 1943.

How many times had I read the inscription above the big doors:

UNION

GOSPEL

TABERNACLE

1891

I knew the interesting story behind the building of this unique "church." Captain Tom Ryman, a hard-drinking owner of a steamboat line, had come to a Sam Jones tent meeting to raise Cain and was soundly converted. In gratitude to God he raised the money for the auditorium that bore his name and dedicated it for evangelistic services. Sam Jones, D. L. Moody, Billy Sunday, J. Wilbur Chapman, and other great preachers of the past had preached here before the building became the home of the "Grand Ole Opry." This night I would pick up the mantle from these great men and proclaim the gospel in old Ryman.

We waited backstage with John and June Cash, our guest artists for the premiere show. At 11:05 P.M. announcer Tom Brown made the station break and during the five-minute network news our choir moved into place on three big risers that had previously been used for John's television show.

The curtain rang up and Tom said, "Good evening, ladies and gentlemen, welcome to the first broadcast of 'Grand Ole Gospel Time,' coming to you live from the stage of the Grand Ole Opry House in Nashville, Tennessee. Here as your host is Pastor Jimmy Snow."

I took the mike and introduced the man the capacity crowd had stayed to hear, Johnny Cash.

The Man in Black was greeted with tumultuous applause. "Take your world and turn it around," he sang in his unique style and the audience cheered and clapped again.

"Jimmy, I've really looked forward to this show going on the air," he ad-libbed. "I really believe you're going to make it big."

The crowd applauded again.

"No radio program is complete until you give a little return to where all good things come from—that's to the Lord."

"Speaking of the Lord, John," I said, "people all over the country are talking about the recent change in your life. I've been reading a book that shows one side of your life, and now I've been privileged for the past year to have seen another side."

"There really was another side, Jimmy. That book covers about seven years, a very miserable seven years. I learned a lot; guess I lived about thirty years in those seven. One thing I did learn is that no matter how hard a man searches for happiness in this world, he can only find it in God. And I had to learn that the hard way."

June Carter joined John on two more songs, backed by the Tennessee Three and the Evangel Temple choir. Then, after the announcer's break, I had seven minutes to preach on "What Think Ye of Christ?" Most of the crowd stayed.

"You must give an opinion," I declared. "You can't wait until you've enjoyed life to the fullest and then think about being saved.

"If you reject Christ tonight, you have crucified Him and put Him to an open shame. . . . You're giving your opinion.

"The moment your opinion is to receive Jesus, that instant you become a child of God.

"You can belong to twenty-five churches and it's not good enough. He can save you tonight if you'll receive Him as your Savior.

"Tonight you can have an experience with God. Like Johnny you can have a new feeling inside of you. If you take Him into your heart, life can change for you. . . ."

The choir began singing softly in the background.

"I'm not asking you to join a church or sign anything. I'm asking if you've got the courage to lift your hand and say, 'Pray for me. I need to be saved.' "

About fifty lifted their hands.

"Now will you go one step further? Come and stand in front of me. There'll be somebody to meet you, show you some Bible verses. Come now. Come."

As prearranged, our choir members were already at the front waiting to counsel those who were coming forward.

The next week Connie Smith was our featured guest.

"It'll be four years in April since I met Jesus," she testified. "I was having trouble in my second marriage, but God allowed it to be that way. . . . I'm glad He was a personal God and reached down and saved my soul. I thank God. I know that big houses and Cadillacs won't satisfy that hunger in your heart. . . . He matters more than anything else in my life."

I preached and more came to accept Jesus.

On subsequent Friday nights we had Marty Robbins, Pat Boone, Bill Monroe, Roy Acuff and other stars. The crowds would stay to hear them and, before they realized it, would be listening to the gospel. I was always careful to stick strictly to the Bible, be brief, and not embarrass WSM and the Opry management. When there was criticism that I was going too far in inviting people to the front during the invitation, I asked seekers to stand where they were and a member of the choir would go and speak to them. The choir members were trained in personal soul winning and could lead people to Christ right in the middle of the auditorium.

"Grand Ole Gospel Time" was a big factor in my determination to stay in the ministry. I knew if I quit the show would fold and thouands of Opry fans would never hear the gospel. I could not go back.

In 1973 we began our second year with "Grand Ole Gospel Time." During the past fifty-two weeks our choir members had personally talked to over two thousand persons who had prayed the sinner's prayer to receive Christ.

The Evangel Temple Christian School was now in its second year with grades kindergarten through sixth. Our plans were to add two grades a year through high school, then start a college.

God sent Harry Yates, an educator from Ohio, to be our principal. Harry hadn't intended to stay in Nashville. Bitter about his divorce and on his way to Texas to drink himself to death, he had stopped only to tell his sister goodbye.

She brought him to Evangel Temple where he found Jesus. What a transformation the Lord made in his life. In no time he was a pillar in the church. When we started the school he was the natural choice for principal.

Harry and I spent a lot of time together while I was going through my divorce trauma. He kept thinking he had seen me somewhere before. One afternoon we were going over some

school plans when he exclaimed, "Now I know. I saw you with
Elvis Presley in 1954 in Lubbock, Texas. You were that pasty-
faced drunk kid leaning on the microphone."

"Yeah, I was there, Harry. I was so stoned out of my mind, I
don't remember going on stage. And here we are serving the
Lord together in Nashville."

Harry found more than salvation and a place of service in
Evangel Tempel. He and Joanne Cash fell in love and were
married in the church. What a beautiful couple they made.
Both starting over again in Jesus and now out in full-time
evangelistic work.

This same year Connie Smith and Marshall Haynes were
married in Evangel Temple. Rex Humbard, the pastor of the
Cathedral of Tomorrow in Akron, Ohio flew down to help me
perform the ceremony.

I knew that many ministers in my denomination wouldn't
officiate at the marriage of a divorced person. What they did
was between them and the Lord, but I felt it was right if the
parties wanted to make a new beginning with God.

For myself, I felt I should not remarry since that would cause
more trouble in the church. I hoped that the commotion cen-
tering around my marital problems would cease.

It was a vain hope. The gossips and scandalmongers wouldn't
let bygones be bygones. Every time I was seen talking to a
woman in a restaurant or on the street, or counseled a woman
alone in my study, a new tale seemed to start. The long
tongues, inside and outside the church, kept the phone lines
hot. "Did you know who I saw with Brother Snow yesterday?"
And, "What do you think about Brother Snow being alone in
his study with ————————?"

No matter that I tried to stay above suspicion. The two single
fellows continued living in my house. I went out to eat with
groups. I made sure that Brenda, whose office was at the other
end of the church, knew who was with me in my study and how
long.

But there was someone else I came to fear more than the dirt peddlers: Myself. I was a virile thirty-seven-year-old male. Human. Subject to temptation. What if I fell after all my protestations of innocence? How could I live with myself, even if the church didn't know?

I was smack in the middle of a music culture where sexual indiscretions are sung about, stimulated, and glorified. I suspected some women of wanting to pull me down to their level, though I never could prove anything.

Maybe my reasoning got twisted—I don't think so, but I reached the place where I felt I would eventually have to remarry or leave the ministry. If I remarried, there would be more defections from the church.

Dottie and I were old friends. She had first married at fifteen and two days later had regretted it. Her second marriage had ended in failure. She had four children, one played the piano and another sang in the choir with her. She herself was one of the most devoted Christians I'd ever known, a person who always seemed to be thinking of others.

Dottie was one of the women tied to me between my separation and divorce. Actually during the months preceding the separation, she was closer to my ex-wife than to me and was crushed to see what was happening between us. She wept and prayed that we would get back together.

Our first "dates," some months after my divorce, were in groups—usually at prayer meetings, church dinners, and the like. Only our very closest friends knew we were interested in each other. When I was at her house, friends or her children were always with us. We were well chaperoned.

After I concluded that I had to remarry or leave the ministry, we began going out discreetly by ourselves. We talked it over, prayed it through, and set a tentative wedding date for the spring of '74. We disagreed on only one aspect. Dottie wanted a church wedding before our children and friends. I feared this would antagonize those in the church who were still upset with me over the divorce, and that a public ceremony would bring more hurtful publicity.

In December I came under heavy pressure. I detected a couple of women making subtle signals in counseling sessions that they were available.

After Christmas, I told Dottie, "Let's go ahead and get married quietly. Once the church knows we've done it, then maybe those who are against my remarriage will accept it."

Dottie felt we should wait but I talked her into doing it my way. We got the license and slipped off like two teenagers and were married outside Nashville on New Year's Eve.

I told the guys living at my house right away. I intended to tell the church the next week. But right after we got back, one of the women who had raised such a fuss about the divorce stormed into my office and announced, "If you get married, my family is gone, and a lot more with us."

The week passed. A month went by. Two months. It was like a soap opera the way we were dodging people and meeting secretly. The gossip was spreading like ragweed.

Crazy? Yes, but I felt trapped. Poor Dottie. I don't know how she took it. Her kids knew about the wedding. My Vanessa didn't. The divorce agreement specified that Vanessa could spend weekends with me. I picked her up at the Opry on Saturday nights and someone from the church took her home Sunday afternoon. She was hearing me preach every Sunday and didn't know I was married again.

I was a coward. I never did make an announcement to the church. In March we just told a couple of people we knew couldn't keep a secret. The next Sunday everybody knew.

The following week one of the ladies of the church came by the house to tell me that God wouldn't use me any longer, now that I had decided to remarry. My anointing would be taken away.

One week before, this same lady had testified in church that God was blessing her life through my ministry more than ever before. Her teenaged son, she had added, who attended Dottie's Sunday school class, was getting closer to God, for which she was very grateful.

Now Dottie and I sat listening to her tell us why such things could no longer happen through us. Finally Dottie reminded her of her previous week's testimony and asked her why God had waited until she found out about our wedding to shed His judgment on me. There was no answer and our conversation soon concluded. After that Dottie saw that God had given us a measure of wisdom in my reluctance to announce our marriage too quickly.

I had already turned in my ordination papers. Technically, this meant I was no longer pastor of Evangel Temple since it was in the denomination.

A special business meeting was called. The constitution required a two-thirds majority vote to take the church out of the denomination. The motion carried. I was still the pastor.

The ones who had opposed my remarriage now left. Some had enough courtesy to tell me why they were leaving. Some simply left their membership cards with Brenda.

Connie Smith's leaving hurt the most. She didn't mention the divorce, remarriage, or denominational issue, but said she wasn't getting fed spiritually. I couldn't understand that, but I appreciated her forthrightness. Connie and her husband and I remain good friends and I boost them every chance I get.

After this third exodus tapered off, attendance bottomed at around two hundred, then started climbing back. I continued getting occasional critical calls which required the utmost patience in answering. All I could say was, "I'm a sinner. But I know God has forgiven me and I still want to serve Him. And I don't feel I should give up and quit because of what happened in the past. I cannot go back."

14
Moving On

Four and a half years have passed since the divorce action was filed; almost three years have gone by since my remarriage. The dust still hasn't settled. I'm still referred to as "that divorced preacher" and Evangel Temple "that divorce mill." To put the record straight about the church: In eleven years there were thirteen divorces within our membership, but because nine of these occurred in 1972, including mine and Connie Smith's, we are called a divorce mill. If the facts were known, I expect that among churches with comparable membership in Nashville, Evangel Temple would be among the lowest.

My reputation and the church's have been tarnished among the self-righteous. But more "sinners" seek us out. They know we aren't a holier-than-thou group sitting in judgment on them.

More come to me for marriage counseling than ever did. Perhaps because the disease of marriage trouble is worse. But some come, I believe, who wouldn't have come to me before. They know I've been through the valley.

It would appear that music people have more marriage

problems than persons in other vocations. I'm not sure that's true, but I do know that show business marriages have unique strains and stresses.

In a typical case a husband might be on the road twenty to thirty days where women are always available, while his wife has remained home with the children. If he doesn't have a tremendous love for his family, an honorable spirit, or a close relationship with God, he will probably yield to temptation. Or his wife may be tempted in her loneliness to drink heavily and run around.

Or there's the situation in which a husband is a star and the wife a plain nobody who is beginning to feel like an appendage. As one Opry wife put it, "People swarm around my husband at parties and I stand there looking dumb."

When the wife is a star and the husband an ordinary working stiff, he feels driven to maintain his self-esteem.

Often two ego-tripping entertainers marry and spend their time trying to up-stage each other.

It's easy for such marriages to crack.

There's another important factor to recognize, peculiar to these permissive times. A performer recently did some very explicit nude scenes in a movie and posed nude with his female lead for a skin magazine. His wife is reportedly very upset. Understandably. Earlier he had come to the altar at Evangel Temple and later had written a hit song for "Grand Ole Gospel Time." It breaks my heart to see such a talented and likeable guy do this. A few years ago it would have been a scandal. Now it's considered chic and a boost to his career. But what will it do to his marriage and the thousands of fans who look up to him?

The permissiveness in country lyrics is hurting. Cheating has always been a theme in country music, but it was never glorified before. Now it seems some writers and performers are following the course set by rock-and-roll.

Understanding the pressures on marriages today helps me

have sympathy for those who have stepped across the line. But this doesn't mean I condone unfaithfulness, nor that I encourage divorce.

I'm a thousand times more against divorce than I ever was. I advise against filing if any love at all remains. I warn that the emotional trauma can tear a family up.

But when it's obvious the relationship is broken beyond the point of no return, I don't insist on any one solution but urge the couple to prayerfully consider their options.

Jesus is our guide here. He heaped woe and damnation on self-serving, judgmental religious hypocrites and showed compassion to sinners.

When the self-righteous Pharisees brought a woman caught in the act of adultery, hoping to trap Jesus, He wrote a message in the sand—perhaps the Ten Commandments. Looking up, He said simply, "He that is without sin among you, let him first cast a stone at her." Then He wrote again—perhaps listing some of their violations of the Commandments, and "being convicted by their own conscience," they "went out one by one." After the last had left, He said to the woman, "Neither do I condemn thee: go, and sin no more" (John 8:3-11).

He was just as forgiving with the Samaritan woman at the well. After hearing about the "living water" He offered, she went out and evangelized her city. Think of that. A five-time loser being used as an evangelist.

Unfortunately, this compassion and forgiveness today is applied only to new Christians. Take myself as an example. Before I was saved I committed almost every sin in the book. Salvation wiped the slate clean and I was welcomed into the church. But fifteen years later when my marriage broke up and I remarried, I became anathema to my denomination. I was supposed to get out of the ministry, eat the dust of my failure. Instead, I have dared to believe that God still wants me in the ministry.

What I now tell Christians who have messed up their lives is this: Seek God's forgiveness. Accept His promise of mercy. Ask for a new filling of the Holy Spirit. Move out. Go forward. If you wait until you're perfect or until all people think well of you, you might as well lie down and die.

I refuse to die. I'm determined to lead my church forward in God's service and let the chips fall where they may.

I've been accused of owning the church. Actually Evangel Temple is governed by a board of trustees, elected by a two-thirds majority of the congregation. They could fire me immediately if they wished.

I've also been charged with profiting from the church. The church pays me $192.50 a week plus utilities, car, and parsonage allowance. From this I must pay child support and support my family.

Rumors persist that I preach heretical doctrine. My sermons are available through a tape ministry. Anyone can get them.

Also that I am no longer Pentecostal. Well, I don't like labels of any kind. And I don't run a circus or do any of the screwball stuff associated with some fringe Pentecostals. When the snakehandlers were making headlines, we announced on our church marquee: NO SNAKES HERE. The picture ran on the front page of the *Nashville Banner* with the caption, "Non-Reptilian Worship."

Critics from another camp say I'm "charismatic." Again, I don't like the label. If this means, do I preach the baptism of the Holy Spirit as Charles Finney and Dwight L. Moody did? Yes. Pray for the sick? Yes, but I don't claim to be a healer nor do I say that it is always God's will to heal. Speak in tongues? Yes, indeed.

Frankly I have some reservations about some so-called charismatics around Nashville. Folks ask me to come to meetings and get turned on by the Spirit. I'm turned off when I don't see the fruit of the Spirit and the separation from the world that the Bible demands. They talk about being "free in the Spirit" from the old legalisms. Well, I don't like some of the old legalisms any more than they do, but if this means free to smoke, drink, dress immodestly, and speak irreverently, then I don't want that kind of freedom. They want to have their cake (the fullness of the Holy Spirit) and eat it too (live like their worldly friends).

At Evangel Temple we try to strike a balance. Be separate without being sanctimonious. Be modest without dressing like you just stepped out of a covered wagon.

The Bible is the core of our curricula in preaching, Sunday school, evangelistic training, Christian growth courses and a weekday school that now reaches through college level. We graduated our first high school class in 1976. A year from now we anticipate our first college commencement with students receiving degrees accredited through Christian University International. We believe Christians should keep learning (Harry Yates and I are working on doctoral degrees) and put their knowledge to work in God's service.

Our dream of becoming a center of Christian training and evangelism is still very much alive. Already, members of Evangel Temple are holding revivals out of state. Harry and Joanne Yates recently held a meeting in California at which over a hundred were saved.

Evangel Temple's corps of singers and personal soul winners will make about ten out-of-town evangelistic trips this year in the church tour bus. I share in the driving, I sing, preach, and give the altar call. The choir members sing and counsel the inquirers.

We just made our tenth visit to the Holy Land and had another baptismal service in the River Jordan. At home I baptize in a nearby lake. Our first builder made the mistake of failing to include a baptistry.

Attendance at Evangel Temple has climbed back to five

hundred. Saturday mornings, our bus workers fan out across Nashville to win souls and enroll new bus riders. Sundays, our fleet of ten buses brings them in.

While we're not the celebrity church we were five years ago, scores of music people still come. Recently half of a six-member rock band and three young women from the Opryland offices came to the Lord.

Every Sunday we have out-of-town visitors. Some heard us on "Grand Ole Gospel Time." Some read about the church in John Cash's book. Some were told by friends this was the church to visit when in Nashville. Among those who have found Christ are a Montana newspaper publisher and his wife and a Congressional aide from Washington, D.C. The aide, Nelson Brown, arranged for me to pray before a session of the House of Representatives. It was on the day Richard Nixon decided to resign from the presidency.

Dad came to church last year for the first time. We cut an LP record for RCA with the Evangel Temple choir before a live audience. It was the first show we had done together in over twenty years.

When he suggested us doing a record, I said, "Okay, if I can write the script as a witness to you." He agreed.

I'm often asked why dad doesn't attend Evangel Temple. My reply is, "He doesn't enjoy being in a crowd where we've had problems with curiosity seekers. The only other reason I can give is that he's just not ready. Dad's one who has to make up his own mind."

But I can say that dad backs me in every other way. He appears on "Grand Ole Gospel Time." And he sends a $300 check every week to the church treasurer.

Our biggest outreach continues to be "Grand Ole Gospel Time" for which I received a special award in 1975 from Religious Heritage of America. For five years, fifty-two Friday night Opries each year, a country-music crowd of two to four thousand and a coast-to-coast radio audience has heard the announcer say, "Welcome to 'Grand Ole Gospel Time,' coming to you live from the stage of the Grand Ole Opry House in Nashville, Tennessee." The show has been broadcast all across Europe and was featured in a series of sixteen TV programs. It's a unique opportunity for which we praise the Lord and thank the Opry management.

Over twelve thousand people have responded to the gospel. We've never asked any to join our church or any other church. But we do send Christian growth material and letters of encouragement to those who record decisions for Christ. And we notify pastors of churches in their vicinity. Joanne Yates is in charge of this ministry.

And we pray for every person by name. After the Friday night Opry we all head back to the church to pray. Evangel Temple may be the only church in the world that holds its regular weekly prayer service at one o'clock, Saturday morning. Most of us will be there for a couple of hours. Some stay until daylight. We go forward on our knees.

Every "Grand Ole Gospel Time" is special, but there is one that will always stand out among the others. It marked the end of an epoch in the history of country music when the Opry moved from Ryman Auditorium to the new $14 million palace in Opryland U.S.A.

Three generations of country performers joined dad and me and the Evangel Temple choir in ringing down the curtain for the last time in Old Ryman. Rosanne Cash, John's daughter; and her sisters, Carlene Smith and Rosie Nix, June's daughters, made their debut with "I Saw the Light." Then the girls joined with John, June, Mother Maybelle Carter, and dad and me in singing the old Carter family favorite, "Will the Circle be Unbroken."

It was almost one A.M. when I began preaching but the Ryman was still jammed. "It's been a long time since Sam Jones came to Nashville and preached hellfire and brimstone to sinners," I said. "A long time since Captain Tom Ryman was converted and inspired to build this old brick tabernacle. I want to preach to you the same gospel that Sam Jones, D. L. Moody, Billy Sunday, and other great voices for God proclaimed from this stage to sinners." Then I took my text from II Corinthians 5:17: "Therefore if any man be in Christ, he is a new creature: old things are passed away; behold, all things are become new." I compared the moving of the Opry to the life-changing experience of salvation.

Then as Jones and Moody and Sunday had done, I invited people to stand. There was a holy hush in the old Gothic church building. A few stood here and there, then with a great rustling hundreds and hundreds joined them while the Evangel Temple choir sang, "Just as I am, without one plea, but that Thy blood was shed for me. . . ."

There were too many standing to count and the aisles were so clogged none could move forward. I asked them to join me in the sinner's prayer: "Jesus, I am a sinner and cannot save myself. I stand on your promise that you will come into my heart. I give myself to you. I love you, Jesus."

And everyone said "amen."

And they did. The word reverberated around the venerable old hall as the last Opry crowd drifted quietly out of the Ryman and an era was ended.

The old Opry stage was transplanted from the Ryman to the new Opry House. Every Friday night when I stand to preach there I'm conscious that this is an epochal event for many of my listeners. They have come from every state and many foreign countries to visit the world-famous Opry. They have stayed for "Grand Ole Gospel Time," which is always included on the Opry program, not expecting to be confronted with an altar call. They may never hear the gospel and be stirred by the Spirit again. It is an awesome feeling to realize that I am God's messenger to them.

When I think of what God has done in my life I am stricken with awe even more. Dad says it is a miracle which should confound all doubters.

It's amazing that after almost two decades, faces still reappear from the past to remind me of what it was like B.C.—Before Christ.

Early last summer a woman with deep lines in her face came up after "Grand Ole Gospel Time" and asked if I remembered her after twenty-one years. "No," I said. "Where did I know you?"

She wiped her eyes. "It was my husband who smashed into your car. I came to the hospital after the wreck and begged you and your parents not to sue."

The years rolled back. "What happened to him?" I asked.

Her voice broke. "After he got out of jail he killed himself."

More recently I was in my study taping remembrances for this book. I had asked that I not be interrupted except for an emergency when Larry Blanton, one of our school teachers, stuck his head in the door. "Pastor, there's a man here who insists he must see you. He's uh, in pretty bad shape."

I shut off the tape recorder and came around the desk to greet a stooped, trembling man who looked about sixty-five.

"Don't you know me, Jimmy?" he sobbed.

I peered at him closely and shook my head.

"From the Greenbriar, the little nightclub on Gallatin Road in Madison. You used to hang out there a lot. I was the manager of the place. Real young for the job. I was just about your age."

I had just turned forty. I thought, "He can't be Billy Wetzel." But he was.

"Jimmy, look at my wrists. I tried to slash them the other day. I got so depressed I just didn't want to live any more."

"Why, Billy?" I asked. "What happened to you?"

"I became an alcoholic after I quit the club. I had a good job at the DuPont plant. They made me a foreman. They gave me chances. Many, many chances. They tried to help me, but I just couldn't break the habit.

"That isn't the worst. After I lost my job, my wife took the children and left. She won't come back. I've begged. I've cried. But she won't. So I took my razor and tried to end my life. A friend found me and saved my life. But if I don't get help, I'll try it again."

I didn't know what to say. The memories were rushing in on me. The times I had tried to do away with myself. The night I put the gun in my mouth.

My eye caught the framed picture of the mailbox on my desk that serves as a reminder of God's mercy to me that cold November night in 1957. There was only one hope for Billy.

We knelt by the office couch. Right in front of the picture of the mailbox Billy sobbed out the sinner's prayer, "O God, have mercy, I'm a sinner. O God, forgive me. O God, save me for Jesus' sake."

After a while he got to his feet. We shook hands.

"Jimmy, a friend is waiting in his car. He drove me over. I lost my license."

"I'm glad you came, Billy. Jesus will help you, just as He helped me."

"I hope so. I meant every word of that prayer. I'll be back."

He started towards the door, then turned around.

"Jimmy, I'm so ashamed. I don't know what good I can ever do. Maybe you can make a sermon about me. Tell young people what drinking can do to a man."

"I'll tell them, Billy."

The next Sunday morning as I related the visit and recalled some of my experiences at the Greenbriar I noticed three women trying to keep from laughing. One was the teacher of our new converts.

Afterwards, the three explained their behavior. "Brother

Snow, when you mentioned the Greenbriar, it struck us funny. We used to go there to drink and dance. Look at us now. Look at you. Isn't it hilariously wonderful what the Lord can do?"

Dottie and the kids were heading toward the car. We have only one car in the family. I had to go into my office and pick up some papers.

I walked in and closed the door for a brief moment. As I stooped to pick up the file folder, I noticed the picture of the mailbox again. The symbol of my deliverance from alcohol and dope and a life of sin.

"Lord, how could I ever go back?"

I turned and saw Brenda's poster. How many times had I been like that defeated young football player sitting with head bowed and helmet in hand, wanting to quit?

But because of the one on the middle cross at the bottom of the poster, the one who didn't quit, I couldn't.

Today I say it again.

I cannot go back.

I cannot quit.

Bruised and battered, I can only go forward. A sinner saved by grace. An unworthy servant called to tell others the good news that only Jesus is the way, the truth, and the life. Nothing else comes close.

Praise God!